APR   9 1997

D0955570

Ready
to
Write

....

World Book, Inc.
a Scott Fetzer company
Chicago   London   Sydney   Toronto

J

Staff

Editorial

**Vice President,
General Publishing**
Dominic J. Miccolis

Administrative Director
Roberta Dimmer

Managing Editor
Maureen Mostyn Liebenson

Permissions Editor
Janet T. Peterson

Contributing Editors
Project developer:
    Joan A. Grygel
Chapter authors:
    Anne M. Eskra
    Philip LeFaivre
    Janice Weiss

Art

Art Director
Wilma Stevens

Senior Editorial Artist
Lisa Buckley

Illustrators
Darryl Kluskowski
Nicholas T. Markell
Cyndy Patrick, cover
illustration

Production Artist
Jim Fuerholzer

Marketing

Product Manager
Amy Moses

Product Production

**Vice President,
Procurement**
Daniel N. Bach

Manufacturing Director
Sandra Van den Broucke

Manager, Manufacturing
Carma Fazio

**Vice President,
Pre-Press Services**
Joseph J. Stack

Production Managers
Barbara Podczerwinski
Madelyn Underwood

Proofreaders
Anne Dillon
Daniel J. Marotta
Joyce Petersen

World Book, Inc.
525 W. Monroe
Chicago, IL 60661

ISBN: 0-7166-2393-5
ISBN: 0-7166-2993-3 (set)
Library of Congress Catalog Card No. 93-60512

Printed in the United States of America

A/IC

Contents

A Note to Parents

Ready to Write is a reference book designed to answer the kinds of questions children ages eight through twelve may have when they are writing stories, essays, letters, or reports. The steps in the writing process lead children from gathering ideas to presenting a final, polished work for sharing with friends or family or for publishing, perhaps in a school or community newspaper. In addition, the writing process is applied to typical school assignments such as writing short reports and answering essay questions.

The purpose behind *Ready to Write* is to help children approach writing with a keen sense of adventure. The book can help children see themselves as writers. It can also help them develop confidence and tune them in to their own creativity as well as sharpen their skills of thinking and communicating clearly. *Ready to Write* supplies children with the tools they need to work on their writing and gives them the power to write well.

This reference book is designed specifically to answer the kinds of questions young writers have about matters such as style, usage, grammar, and types of writing. The in-depth coverage of these topics makes the book appropriate for increasingly sophisticated writers. For example, younger writers may have questions about end-of-sentence punctuation marks while more mature writers will want to see appropriate punctuation examples for their more-complex writing structures. The broad range of topics makes *Ready to Write* a reference that young writers will not quickly outgrow. The information is easily accessible and is presented in a user-friendly format that includes clear explanations and informative examples.

Join your child in the adventure that is writing by being an appreciative audience. Discover together the world of unique ideas your child expresses through writing. By presenting your child with *Ready to Write*, you have opened the door to a wealth of opportunities that come through well-crafted communication.

A Note to the Writers Who Use This Book

While you're writing, you're probably thinking about two things at once—*what* you're writing about and *how* your writing is going. *Ready to Write* is a book to dip into as you have questions about the *how* part of writing. Take a few minutes to flip through this book. You'll see that there are lots of helps for answering your "How do I . . . " questions. To answer your questions even faster, take a look at the types of help you'll find throughout the chapters:

Important words are printed in **heavy, black type.**

Examples of writing are set off like this.

Sometimes the examples include **Before** and **After** to show how a writer changed his or her writing.

$\mathcal{P}$ A magnifying glass shows a list of ideas you will want to read closely.

> Lists or longer examples are in colored blocks like this.

☞ Sometimes more help appears in another place in the book.

☐ Checklists help you look over your writing and make sure you've remembered to do certain things.

Of course, to find a piece of information fast, you can use the table of contents at the front of this book.

Skim through *Ready to Write* before you begin to write. Then use it whenever you have a "How do I . . ." question. It's like having a knowing friend right at your fingertips.

A LOOK AT THE
WRITING
PROCESS

Why write? What if:

> Your teacher assigned a book report. It's due in a week.

> The mayor is talking about closing your favorite playground. You'd like to write a letter to the newspaper, explaining how important that playground is to you and your friends.

> Your grandmother sent you a great birthday present. You want to write her a thank-you note.

These three writing tasks are very different. But in one way, they're similar. Whether you're writing a book report, a letter to a newspaper, or a thank-you note, you must go through the same steps to get from start to finish. Those steps are called the **writing process.**

On the next pages you'll see a diagram of the steps in the writing process. Any writing task will be easier if you follow these steps.

The Writing Process

Planning

Think about why you are writing. (Purpose)
Think about who will read your writing. (Audience)
Think about your subject. (Topic)
Choose ideas to write about. (Content)
Decide how to organize your ideas. (Organization)

Drafting (Sitting down and writing)

Think about how to present your information. How will you organize your points?

Write a **draft**—a first version of what you want to say. *Do* put all your ideas down on paper.

Don't worry about spelling or punctuation.

Do use sentences and paragraphs.

Writing
2

When you plan your writing, you let the ideas flow. Then you decide which ones you will actually use and arrange them in order. While you are drafting, work only on getting your ideas down on paper. *Do not* stop to read what you wrote, look up spellings, or fix sentences. Just keep the writing flow going.

As you reread your draft, pretend you're a reader seeing it for the first time and try to imagine what a reader would think. You also might ask a reader for feedback. Then ask yourself the questions under *Revising.*

If you're like most writers, you'll probably decide to make some changes. You might want to say something differently, you might have a new idea to put in, or you might want to take out something.

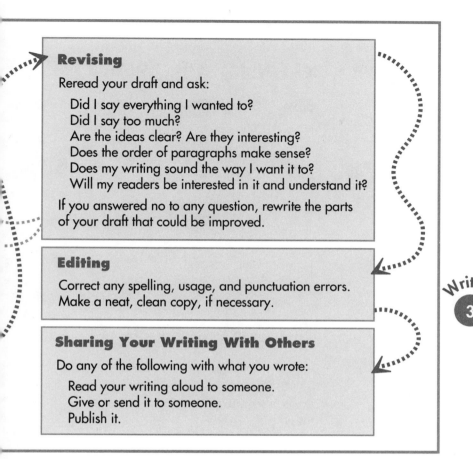

Revising

Reread your draft and ask:

Did I say everything I wanted to?
Did I say too much?
Are the ideas clear? Are they interesting?
Does the order of paragraphs make sense?
Does my writing sound the way I want it to?
Will my readers be interested in it and understand it?

If you answered no to any question, rewrite the parts of your draft that could be improved.

Editing

Correct any spelling, usage, and punctuation errors.
Make a neat, clean copy, if necessary.

Sharing Your Writing With Others

Do any of the following with what you wrote:

Read your writing aloud to someone.
Give or send it to someone.
Publish it.

Writing
3

So you back up and rewrite part of your draft, or add something new, or . . . just start over! That's the revising step. Revising can take you back to planning, back to drafting, or forward to editing.

If you decide to revise, does that mean you did something wrong? No! It just shows that reading your draft made you think about what you said and how you said it. Don't be surprised if you change your mind.

Once you have a draft that you're happy with, you're ready to edit it. That's not the same as revising. Editing means correcting errors and putting on the final "polish" that will make your writing shine!

Chapters 1 through 4 (pages 8-95) explain the steps of the writing process in greater detail.

KEEPING A PERSONAL
JOURNAL

Journal
4

Which of these feelings have you had?

> excited because something fantastic just happened
>
> furious because someone treated you unfairly
>
> sad because you're losing a friend

Most of us have had these feelings and many others. Sometimes we share our feelings with people we're close to, and other times we just keep them inside.

Have you ever tried writing in a personal journal when you're bursting with feelings or ideas? It's like sharing with a good friend who listens *only* to you—and who never interrupts.

What's a journal? It's a place where you write or draw about whatever is on your mind. You can record events or ideas or feelings or problems or whatever *you* want. You don't have to use your journal every day if you don't feel like it.

Keeping a journal can make you feel better if something is bothering you. It can help you figure out ways to handle problems. Sometimes it can give you ideas you'd like to write about later and share with others.

Here are some examples from young people's journals. This first one was written by Dan, age 10, while on a trip with his family:

We went on a tour of the White House. It was awesome! I kept hoping we'd see the President, but we didn't. Anyway, we saw a lot of the fancy rooms where the First Family has big dinners and stuff like that. There were guards all over the place. After the tour we saw a helicopter land on the White House lawn. We found out later it was picking up the President! But we couldn't see him.

Here's some journal writing by Ellen, age 12. How do you think she was feeling when she wrote this?

Tryouts for the class play are tomorrow. I really want to get a good part, but I doubt it's going to happen. Mrs. Norton says anyone who tries out can make it, but I really want to do more than just the chorus. Katie and Alison are trying out too. I think they're much better than I am. I don't think I stand much of a chance for a big part.

The next journal entry was written by Marshall, age 11. Why did he make this entry?

It makes me so MAD when Tyrone gets to do things I never could when I was his age! Mom says he's not the same kind of kid as I was. What difference does that make? It's not FAIR! She didn't let me go to the arcade alone when I was 10. Ty's only 10, and she lets him go alone all the time.

As you see, you can express *anything* in a personal journal. It's like a secret friend with whom you can share your thoughts and feelings.

A journal can also be more than a record of your thoughts, feelings, or experiences. It can help you explore ideas you might want to write more about later. For instance, Marshall's teacher might ask the class to write a piece that convinces someone to do something. Marshall might decide to write about why parents should be fair with their children.

Ellen might write a story about friends who try out for a play and how they feel about the outcome. Dan might want to write a special "travel story" about his visit to the White House for his school newspaper.

Just remember—your journal is *yours.* You can write in it whenever you want, whatever you want, and however you want. You can read it whenever you want. You can even keep a list of topics you'd like to write about or ideas for stories.

CHAPTER ONE
PLANNING

Do you want to submit your favorite joke to a magazine? Did your teacher ask you to write an adventure tale? Do you need to leave a note for your neighbor explaining how to care for your fish while you're away?

Why Are You Writing?

You may write for one special reason or for a combination of reasons. The type of writing you do depends on your reasons for writing. Most writing tries to do just a few basic things, as the following sections explain.

Writing to Tell a Story

Some writing starts with your imagination. This is called **fiction writing.** Some fiction is very different from real life. A reader can tell that it could not really happen or be true. Read this example:

> The strange, shimmering object hung in the air over the parking lot. I felt drawn by its low, humming sound. The eerie way it changed colors wasn't like anything I had ever seen. It opened, and a dragonfly-shaped being floated out.

Although it is made up, fiction also may tell of events or people that seem as if they could be real. Here is an example of realistic fiction:

> Lola ran to the window just in time to see her father driving away. She hoped he wouldn't get back before she hung his "Happy Birthday" banner.

Writing to Tell about an Experience

Writing often tells about events that really have happened. When you write about your day or about a football game you played, for example, you are writing a **narrative.**

We moved into our new apartment last weekend. It was unsettling! First, we had to pack up everything in the old apartment. That took about a week and put everybody in a grumpy mood. Unpacking was no picnic either.

Writing to Describe

Descriptive writing paints word pictures of people, places, or things. It is so detailed that a reader knows exactly how something looks—or how it sounds, feels, smells, or tastes.

Planning
10

My hamster, Snoozy, is a warm, velvety ball of sleepy brown-and-white fur by day. But at night he scampers around his cage as if he's working out with an exercise tape on fast speed. What a bouncy bundle of energy! Sometimes I think he should have two names— Snoozy by day and Peppy at night.

My favorite meal at any time of the day is pizza. I love the wonderful smell of the dough slowly browning in the oven and the tangy scent of tomato sauce. Then I relish feeling the cheese str-r-r-retch when I bite into it.

Writing to Explain

Sometimes you will write to answer questions such as these:

- Who or what is this person or thing?
- Why is this person or thing important?
- What does this person or thing do?
- How does this thing work?

Read these examples of writing that explains:

> Paper must be broken down to be recycled. First it is torn into tiny pieces. Next it is soaked in water until it dissolves. Then the water is squeezed out. Now the leftover pulp can be formed into new paper.

> My grandmother is a very important person in my life. If my parents are busy or aren't at home, I like to call or visit her. She's usually at home, and we have a good time talking about what's going on.

Writing to Convince the Reader

Writers sometimes want to convince readers to do something or to share an opinion about something. But it's not enough to say simply: "Do this!" or "Think like me!" Writers must state reasons and facts that back up, or support, their points of view.

> I nominate Mr. John Cummings for Holmes School Teacher of the Year. Mr. Cummings knows how to make all his students think, and he never makes anyone feel bad. He presents information in an interesting way, and he makes sure everyone understands before he goes on to something new. Most important, he always keeps his sense of humor.

Writing a Friendly Letter

If you've ever gotten mail, you know how much fun it is to find a letter just for you in your mailbox. Your friends and relatives probably feel the same about getting a letter from you!

> Dear Dave,
>
> Are you coming to the family reunion next month? So far, about thirty people are coming. Uncle Jack is bringing his new cocker spaniel. He says it's really friendly, but it's not housebroken yet. I hope you're coming!
>
> Your cousin,
> Roger

☞ **Writing a Short Report,** pages 102–116.

Writing to Complete Assignments

Have you ever written a book report for school, or a report about information that you looked up in a book or magazine? Reports can describe, explain, or try to convince. It all depends on the assignment.

Writing to Answer Test Questions

☞ **Answering Essay Questions,** pages 116–119.

Sometimes test questions must be answered in complete sentences or in paragraphs. The question may ask you to summarize, describe, explain, or convince.

Who Will Read Your Writing?

Your friend asks, "Are you having tuna casserole for lunch?" You answer, "Yuck! I *hate* that stuff!" But what if the cafeteria server asks you the same question? Then you might say a polite, "No, thank you."

Why would you give different answers to the same question? Most of us speak a little differently depending on to whom we're speaking. The same thing is true when writing. Are you writing for adults? Then you probably will be more formal and serious than if your readers were your friends. You also will be more formal if your reader doesn't know you—for instance, if you're writing a letter to your new pen pal.

When you write, you also need to consider how much your reader already knows about your subject. Let's say you're writing about how to make a free throw in basketball. If your reader knows something about the game, you don't need to explain what the key is. But, if the reader isn't familiar with the game, you'll have more explaining to do.

How Can You Get Ideas for Writing?

Do you have a writing assignment, but the ideas just won't come? Don't give up! There are many ways to find ideas and focus on a topic for writing.

Getting Ideas from Drawing

Suppose you're going to make up a story about a fishing trip, but you're not sure where to start. Try drawing a picture of what you imagine. That will help you "see" details you can include in your writing. (Don't worry—it doesn't have to be great art!)

Getting Ideas from Freewriting

You may think you have no ideas to write about. But that's not true! Ideas are bouncing around in your head all the time. Try freewriting to tap into them. **Freewriting** means writing whatever comes into your mind. You write without stopping for five minutes or so. It may look like a jumble, but you can uncover gems of ideas to develop in your writing.

Planning
14

I don't know what to write about, but here goes—5 minutes—long time! Oh yeah! I've got to get my watch fixed -- bike needs air in tires too—why? How does air escape if there's no hole? Skateboarding's better — no maintenance — no tires — but not as safe — need safety stuff: knee pads, wrist pads, elbow pads, and helmet.

Getting Ideas from Brainstorming

Try brainstorming when you have lots of ideas but aren't sure where to start, what to include, or what to leave out. **Brainstorming** just means jotting down ideas freely as they come to you, without deciding whether or how they fit together. It lets you put *lots* of ideas on paper so you have plenty to choose from.

Following is the brainstorming of a student who wanted to write about environmental problems.

ENVIRONMENT

oil spills   plastic
animals killed   land fills
messy beaches   watershortage
clean-upss sprinklers in Arizona
car exhaust   solar energy
dirty air   solar collectors
public transportation   Biosphere
recycling Wood burning stoves
waste paper save the forests

Getting Ideas from Reading Books and Your Journal

A book can give you new and interesting ideas. Perhaps you read a book about a person who survived alone in the wilderness. It might start you thinking: "What would I do in the same situation?" Or you might imagine yourself on an adventure. Where would you go? What would you do? Think about books you've read. What other writing ideas might books give you?

Your journal might help, too. Leaf through it. Which experience, problem, or friend might be a topic for writing? Maybe you could write some realistic fiction based on something that's happened to you.

Getting Ideas from Charting

Sometimes making a chart can help you think through a subject. Making a chart of causes and effects, comparisons and contrasts, or pros and cons can bring out details. Remember the brainstorming example about environmental problems? The following writer decided to group her ideas into causes and effects.

CAUSES	EFFECTS
oil spills	animals killed
	land dirty
	water dirty
engine exhaust	air pollution
forest cutting	land erosion
	water cycle harmed
	lose natural growth
	animals killed

Getting Ideas from Mapping

Mapping is another way to come up with additional ideas for a topic. The secret is to put your main idea in the center and ask yourself questions about it. Then connect answers to your questions, or group the ideas with lines, circles, or some other design.

Page 17 shows two different maps an eleven-year-old made of her ideas about unhealthy food.

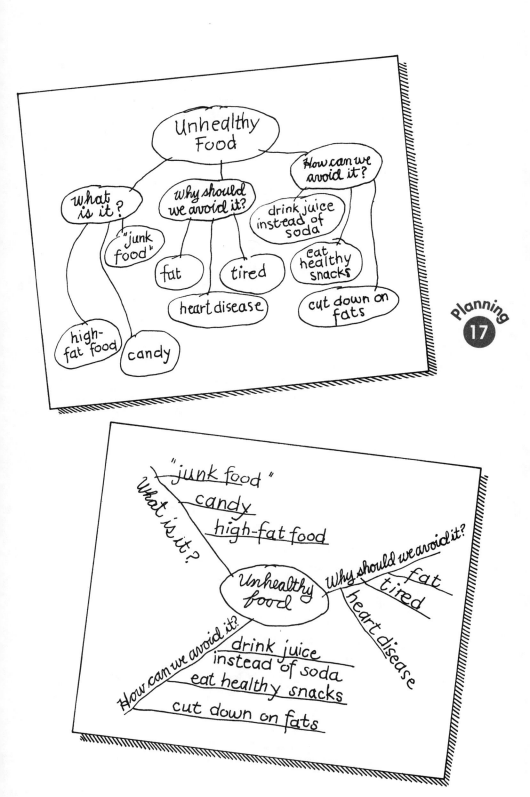

☞ Finding
Information
for Your
Report,
pages
106–111.

Getting Ideas from Research

Finally, you can always turn to encyclopedias, other informational books, or magazines to learn about a subject.

How Can You Use Your Ideas?

Skim over your ideas. Now it's time to evaluate them. If you have several topics, you'll need to choose one. Then you can do some mapping or charting for details. But what if you have too many details? What if the details don't fit together in any way? What do you do next?

Narrowing Your Topic

At this point, you'll need to decide which of your ideas you want to write about. For example, look again at the map about healthful food. Using everything in the map would mean researching many topics to develop all of those ideas, and you could write a book! Therefore, you would have to **narrow the topic**—that is, choose one part of the subject.

From the broad subject *unhealthy food*, you might choose a topic such as *how unhealthy food affects us, the most popular unhealthy foods*, or *how to eat a healthy diet*. You could find information on any of these topics to write a report. As you can see, it is best to narrow a topic before researching it.

Look again at the freewriting sample on page 14. It might lead you to write about sports. That's a broad topic. Here's how you might narrow it:

Broad topic:	sports
Narrow topic:	sporting equipment
Narrower topic:	safety equipment in sports
Narrowest topic:	safety equipment for skate-boarding

Developing Your Ideas

What if you're not sure you have *enough* things to say about your topic? Then spend some time coming up with more ideas. In addition to getting ideas and details by charting or mapping, see if some of the suggestions that follow make sense for your subject and type of writing.

If you want to tell a story, you'll probably want to write about events in **time order.** Start by describing the first event, then the next, and so on. Here's an example:

Event 1▸ On the morning of the big storm, I woke up to gray clouds churning across the sky.

Event 2▸ By the time I went down for breakfast, rain was slapping against the window.

Event 3▸ I jumped when lightning flashed and thunder boomed across the countryside.

You can use time order if you want to explain how something works, too. For example:

Paper must be broken down to be recycled.

Event 1▸ *First* it is torn into tiny pieces.

Event 2▸ *Next* it is soaked in water until it dissolves.

Event 3▸ *Then* the water is squeezed out.

Event 4▸ *Now* the leftover pulp can be formed into new paper.

If you want to describe or explain something, you should **list details** about it or **give examples** of it. Here's another paragraph you read earlier. Notice the details it presents.

> My favorite meal at any time of the day is pizza.
>
> **Detail 1►** I love the *wonderful smell of the dough* slowly browning in the oven
>
> **Detail 2►** and the *tangy scent of tomato sauce.*
>
> **Detail 3►** Then I relish feeling the *cheese str-r-r-retch* when I bite into it.

If you're trying to convince a reader, **list reasons** to back up your argument with supporting details.

> I nominate Mr. John Cummings for Holmes School Teacher of the Year.
>
> **Reason 1►** Mr. Cummings *knows how to make all his students think,*
>
> **Reason 2►** and he *never makes anyone feel bad.*
>
> **Reason 3►** He *presents information in an interesting way,*
>
> **Reason 4►** and he *makes sure everyone understands* before he goes on to something new.
>
> **Reason 5►** Most important, he *always keeps his sense of humor.*

As you see, focusing on *why* you're writing helps you think of the supporting details you should include. Once you've developed your ideas in this way, you're ready to write your draft!

CHAPTER TWO

DRAFTING

When you planned your writing, you decided on the purpose, topic, audience, and basic content. In a way, you are like a person building a home. You've planned what kind of home you will build. You've chosen the location and gathered bricks, boards, pipes, and wire. Now it's time to build. The suggestions in this chapter will help you make sure you have everything you need and show you how to build your draft.

Tap into the ideas floating in your head and get them down on paper before you forget something. That's what drafting is all about. You can add the finishing touches later.

Drafting a Paragraph

When you're building your draft, think of the words as boards, the sentences as rooms, and the paragraphs as floors or stories of a building. A **paragraph** is a group of sentences that expresses one idea or purpose. Start by asking yourself, "What's the main idea I want to make in this paragraph?" Write that idea in one sentence. That's called a **topic sentence**. It states the main idea of your paragraph, and it usually comes first in the paragraph.

Then, write some sentences that build on the main idea. Make sure they all explain or tell more about your topic sentence. If they don't, they don't belong in the paragraph!

Now, write a **concluding sentence** summing up your main idea in new words. If your paragraph told a story, the concluding sentence should add an end to your story.

Topic Sentence — My best friend Matt and I have several things in common. We both love performing magic tricks. We also like to play basketball. Since Matt has a crazy sense of humor and I love to laugh, we always tell each other jokes. No wonder Matt and I have been buddies since kindergarten! — **Concluding Sentence**

Drafting a Longer Piece of Writing

Building a longer piece of writing is like adding floors to build a skyscraper. If you're writing a piece consisting of three paragraphs or more, you first decide on the main idea you want to get across. State it in a **thesis sentence.** Here are some examples:

Drafting 23

> My family's camping trip last summer was the best vacation I've ever had.

> Driving out of Chicago on Route I-94 gives a great view of the big city.

> I think allowances should be based on how much children help around the house.

Write your thesis sentence in the first paragraph, or **introduction,** of your piece. Use the rest of that paragraph to get your readers' attention. How? That's up to you. You can tell part of your story, describe your subject a bit, or explain why the subject interests you.

> My family's camping trip last summer was the best vacation I've ever had. Of course, I could have skipped the long, boring hours driving on the turnpike and the cold nights spent shivering in a sleeping bag. But the campfire stories in the rolling green hills of Vermont made it all worthwhile.

After the introductory paragraph comes the **body,** or main part, of your piece. Here you present the facts, examples, details, or reasons that support the thesis statement. Be sure each paragraph has one main idea. Be sure, too, that every sentence in the paragraph tells about it. Then put the paragraphs in the body in an order that makes sense.

The last part is the **concluding paragraph.** Here you can restate the idea of your thesis sentence or sum up the experience you wrote about. Either way, the last paragraph should *feel* like an ending that ties things together. Try to include a sentence that will stick in your readers' minds. Here's an example:

> If you want a bird's-eye view of my home city, try cruising down I-94. The houses, buses, trains, factories, bridges, billboards, and bustling streets of Chicago will be spread out all around you!

Drafting Different Kinds of Writing

What should you include? It depends on your reason for writing. Do you want to tell a story or explain how to do something? Your "building" will be different for each writing purpose.

Telling a Story

Let's say you want to write a story from your imagination. All stories have a few things in common.

Characters. Your story will be about people, animals, or made-up beings. These are the **characters.** You may want to describe some of them in detail and others only a little. You'll want to bring your characters to life in your readers' minds. Help them understand *why* your characters do what they do.

Setting. The place where a story happens is its **setting.** Describe your story's setting with vivid details to help your readers "see" it clearly and feel as if they are there.

> Darkness was quickly falling in the for-
> est. The bare trees trembled and creaked
> in the cold wind. On the ground, dry
> leaves whispered softly in the shadows.

Plot. What will happen in your story? Together, the events of a story are called the **plot.** Don't leave out any important parts, or you may confuse your readers! Be sure to put the events in an order that makes sense. That probably will be time order, from the earliest event to the latest one.

Dialogue. In most stories, characters talk to each other. Their conversation is called **dialogue.** Imagine how your characters would actually talk, and write the dialogue to make your story seem more real.

Tension. Usually, a story contains some kind of **tension.** A problem must be solved, a danger lurks, or something good or bad is about to happen. Because of the tension, your characters may feel nervous and worried or happy and excited. Describe your characters and events clearly. If you use vivid detail, your readers will feel the tension, too. Make your readers feel that they can't wait to find out what happens next or how the story ends.

Climax. The moment the most important event happens is called the **climax.** That's when the writer finally relieves the tension and answers the question, "What's going to happen?" Be sure the climax explains clearly and believably just how things work out in your story.

Telling about an Experience

People often write about an experience they've had or an event they know about. Most experiences actually include several events. The phone rings, you run to answer it, you trip on the rug, and . . . you break your mother's favorite lamp! Be sure to describe all the important events so your readers will understand just what happened.

In some ways, writing about an experience can be like writing a story. That's because an experience may also include a setting, people, and dialogue. You can describe people and settings just as you would in a story. Use some dialogue if you remember it—or if you remember more or less what it was. Good dialogue can make writing come alive.

> "You've got to be kidding," Alex said. "You? In ballet shoes?" He laughed, then shook his head, muttering, "*This* I've got to see."

You'll probably want to describe the events in time order, starting with the earliest event and ending with the latest one. Sometimes when you're telling about an experience, you might want to jump back to an earlier event. In other words, you move backward in time, or include a **flashback.**

> As I stepped into the spotlight in the final act of the show, I thought back to that day in second grade when I first tried ballet in gym class. I remembered my buddy Alex laughing at me when I tried to twirl on my toes. I felt proud that Alex wasn't laughing at me any more.

Sometimes, though, you might want to surprise your readers by jumping forward in your story to a "late" event—maybe the most exciting one. This is called a **flash-forward.** Here's an example:

> I looked into the audience and suddenly felt as unsteady as a newborn colt. If I'd known then that the entire audience would rise to its feet and applaud me, I might have been less nervous. But all I could think was that I had to remember *all* the ballet steps *and* not fall off the edge of the stage! I just wanted my dance to be over with as quickly as possible. In fact, I wished they'd turn off the lights so no one could see me.

Describing

Do you want to paint a word picture of a person, place, or thing? Then include the details that make your subject special. Let your senses help you. Ask yourself, "How does this thing (or this person) look, feel, smell, sound, and maybe even taste?"

Make the details as clear and specific as you can. Don't just say a *bike* if it's really a beat-up old bike with bent spokes and one rusty fender. Don't just say a *chocolate sundae* if it's really a tall mound of luscious vanilla ice cream with deep, dark chocolate gently dribbling down the sides. Clear, strong details give sharp focus to your "word picture." They help the readers "see" your subject as you do.

☞ **Elaboration, page 52.**

You also might organize your ideas as if you were filming the thing you describe. Do you want to film it looking from the inside to the outside? You also could describe it from far away and gradually get closer. Sometimes you might want to give a bird's-eye view, from the top down. All of these are examples of different **points of view.**

Explaining

At times you may write to explain something. You might need to explain how plants make food from air, sunshine, and water. Or maybe you need to explain how the Thanksgiving holiday first began.

What main idea do you want to get across? Write it in one sentence. Put it at the beginning of your piece as a thesis sentence.

Thesis **sentence, page 23.**

> In the last few years, people have begun recycling many things instead of tossing them into garbage dumps.

> Plants have an amazing ability to make their own food, using only air, sunshine, and water.

To explain your subject, you may need to define a term. For example, in a piece about recycling you may need to explain what *recycling* means. Think about what your readers may not know or understand.

Examples help explain things, too. Can you describe some examples of things that are recycled? They will help your readers understand the process.

Sometimes explaining covers a series of events. Imagine you're writing about how to bake bread. You'll need to tell how to measure the ingredients, mix them, knead the dough, and so on. Be sure to tell the events in the correct order. If you're explaining how one thing causes another, make clear which comes first and which is the result.

Convincing the Reader

When you are building a draft to convince readers to act or believe in a certain way, you are expressing an **opinion**—what you feel or believe. You must be very considerate of your readers, because they have opinions, too. First, you show the readers that

Drafting 29

you understand the facts about the issue. **Facts** are something that can be proved; everyone agrees on their truth. You might try starting with the least important fact and ending with the most important.

> In Mayfair Park four of the six swings are hanging by rusty chains that may break at any time. The slide is dented in many places and has a dangerous sharp edge at the bottom. In the past month, four children have hurt themselves on it.

Then, you present your opinion. Show that you realize others may disagree with you. Don't make fun of readers' opinions, but treat them with respect.

> I believe the city government should buy new equipment for this park. I know the government has little extra money to spend. Our officials have to make hard decisions about what we can afford. But I believe the children of our city deserve to have safe places to play.

Writing a Letter

A letter to a friend can include just about anything! That's what makes it fun to write. In general, though, people usually include a few features in all personal letters.

The **heading** is the part of the letter that gives your address and the date. Write it at the top, even with the left margin, or in the right-hand corner of your letter.

The **salutation,** or greeting, begins the letter. It starts at the left margin and ends with a comma.

The **body** is the main part of the letter. That's where you say everything you want your reader to know. Start the body just under the salutation. Indent the first line as you would indent a paragraph. If the body contains more than three or four sentences, make separate paragraphs.

☞ Drafting a Paragraph, page 22.

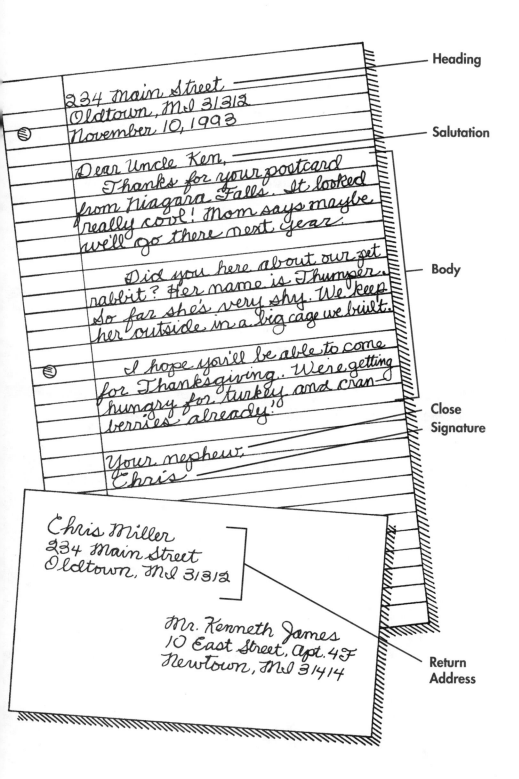

Heading

234 Main Street
Oldtown, MI 31312
November 10, 1993

Salutation

Dear Uncle Ken,
    Thanks for your postcard
from Niagara Falls. It looked
really cool! Mom says maybe
we'll go there next year.

Body

    Did you here about our pet
rabbit? Her name is Thumper.
So far she's very shy. We keep
her outside in a big cage we built.

    I hope you'll be able to come
for Thanksgiving. We're getting
hungry for turkey and cran-
berries already!

Close
Signature

Your nephew,
Chris

Chris Miller
234 Main Street
Oldtown, MI 31312

Mr. Kenneth James
10 East Street, Apt. 4F
Newtown, MI 31414

Return Address

Bring the letter to an end with a **close** such as *Yours truly, Your friend,* or *Sincerely.* Line it up with the heading.

Write your **signature,** or name, under the close. Line it up with the first word of the close.

Address the envelope in your neatest handwriting so your letter will get to the right place. Write the **return address**—your name and address—in the upper left-hand corner. If the letter can't be delivered, it will be returned to you.

Write the name and address of the person to whom you're writing in the center of the envelope, a little below the middle. Put the name on the first line and the street address on the second. If there's an apartment number, write it after the street. On the third line, write the person's city, state, and ZIP code. Use the two-letter abbreviation for the state.

Two-letter Postal Abbreviations

Alabama	AL	Kentucky	KY	Ohio	OH
Alaska	AK	Louisiana	LA	Oklahoma	OK
Arizona	AZ	Maine	ME	Oregon	OR
Arkansas	AR	Maryland	MD	Pennsylvania	PA
California	CA	Massachusetts	MA	Rhode Island	RI
Colorado	CO	Michigan	MI	South Carolina	SC
Connecticut	CT	Minnesota	MN	South Dakota	SD
Delaware	DE	Mississippi	MS	Tennessee	TN
District of		Missouri	MO	Texas	TX
Columbia	DC	Montana	MT	Utah	UT
Florida	FL	Nebraska	NE	Vermont	VT
Georgia	GA	Nevada	NV	Virginia	VA
Hawaii	HI	New Hampshire	NH	Washington	WA
Idaho	ID	New Jersey	NJ	West Virginia	WV
Illinois	IL	New Mexico	NM	Wisconsin	WI
Indiana	IN	New York	NY	Wyoming	WY
Iowa	IA	North Carolina	NC		
Kansas	KS	North Dakota	ND		

CHAPTER THREE
REVISING

As you wrote your draft, you were recording any thoughts that came to mind. You didn't pay attention to the way they sounded, if they made sense, or even if they were exactly what you wanted to say. Think of revising as tending a garden. You may have to pull some weeds or replant bare spots.

You **revise** to make sure that you've said what you want to say in a way that you want to say it. Revising is the time for you to look at your draft as if you were the reader, not the writer.

☞ **A Look at the Writing Process, pages 1–3.**

When you've finished drafting, wait at least a day before revising. Then read your writing as if you were a reader who hadn't seen it before. One good trick is to try reading it aloud to yourself. Sometimes saying the words aloud helps you to hear something you'll want to change. Also, a friend or family member could read it and make suggestions.

Make notes and ask questions that another reader might ask. You'll probably find yourself marking places that are confusing, unclear, or perhaps a bit awkward. Using proofreader's marks speeds up the process of revising and editing. In fact, a pair of scissors and some paste can be handy tools if you decide to rearrange large sections. Don't worry about making a mess—you can recopy your final product later.

☞ **Proofreader's Marks, page 93.**

In revising you'll be looking at:

○ the content (what you included),

○ the particular words you used and the way sentences and paragraphs fit together, and

○ your writing style (the *you* readers meet through your writing).

These three areas of revising are handled separately in this chapter. However, like the writing process itself, you'll probably jump back and forth among them as certain things catch your eye or your ear.

Revising Content

Drafting ✎
**Different Kinds
of Writing,
pages 25–30.**

One of the first things you'll notice as you read your draft is which ideas you included. These ideas came from your planning, and they depend on the kind of writing you are doing. As you revise, you may want to look at your planning ideas again.

Following is a draft of the beginning of a report. In this example, the writer has the ideas down on paper, but the draft sounds more like a list of facts than like finished writing. You probably can see many improvements the writer could make.

> The catfish is like other fish but different. There are more than 2,000 separate species of catfish. There are 30 different families of catfish. Catfish look like cats because they have whiskers. Both cats and catfish are vertebrates. Catfish are cold-blooded. Fishers catch catfish with dough balls.

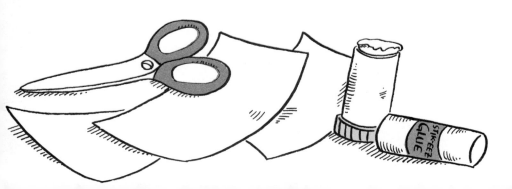

Thinking as your readers might, ask yourself the following questions:

○ Will readers understand any special terms used? In the catfish report readers may not know *species, families,* and *vertebrates.* Including **definitions** might help.

○ Would adding information make the content clearer? In the catfish paragraph, perhaps the writer should give some **examples** of cold-blooded animals.

☞ **Narrowing Your Topic, page 18.**

○ Is there too much information? Maybe narrowing the topic a bit or **removing** some sentences would help. For example, the sentence about catching catfish could be removed (or moved to another paragraph if fishing is part of the topic).

○ If you **rearrange the order,** will it be easier for readers to follow your thinking? The first sentence in the catfish example leads readers to believe the paragraph will be about how catfish are like or different from other fish. The sentences comparing cats and catfish are out of place—they could be made into a separate paragraph about how catfish got their name.

Using the Right Word

A famous writer, Mark Twain, once said, "The difference between the *almost right* word and the right word is really a large matter—it's the difference between the lightning bug and the lightning."

When you revise, you can look for places to use "lightning"

words or details that make your writing light up the readers' minds. Look at the following description:

> The worker was tired. He lifted the load
> to his shoulder again and went down the
> road.

This writing has strong feeling, but it doesn't create a very clear picture. You could improve it by replacing vague or imprecise words with more specific, accurate, or colorful ones or by adding some details.

> The *bricklayer* was *exhausted*. He lifted
> the *bundle* onto his shoulder *once more*
> and *trudged* down the road.

Synonyms and Antonyms

One way to strike lightning with words is by using synonyms. **Synonyms** are two or more words that mean almost the same thing. For example, *tired, exhausted,* and *weary* are synonyms.

You might want to improve your writing by making a sharp contrast between two ideas. In that case you could use a word that means the opposite of another, or an **antonym.** *Under* and *over* are antonym pairs. It matters very much which antonym you use, as the following example shows:

> On the third day, the pioneers passed
> through a long valley that was green and
> *broad/narrow.* In it they encountered
> *clear/hazy* weather and *many/few* animals. They ate so *much/little* that they
> were *full/hungry.* After that, their mood
> was one of *hope/despair.*

Although a word may have many synonyms, sometimes it has only one or two antonyms. Words that have more than one meaning may have synonyms or antonyms for each meaning. Look at the antonyms for *light*.

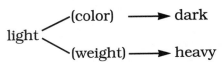

Using a Thesaurus. You can find synonyms and antonyms for many words in a reference book called a **thesaurus.** Here is a sample entry for the word *fat*.

Revising
38

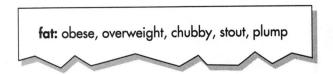

fat: obese, overweight, chubby, stout, plump

☞ Using a Dictionary, pages 45–46.

Denotation and Connotation. The **denotation** is the dictionary, or literal, meaning of a word. When you decide among synonyms, you may base your decision on different shades of meaning, or **connotations.**

Look again at the thesaurus entry. Suppose you have written *The clown was fat* and want to replace the word *fat* with a clearer word. All of the synonyms have the same or a similar denotation: "having a type of white or yellow oily substance found in the body of animals." The connotations of each of these words are very different. *Obese* is a word for what doctors describe as being very fat; *overweight* suggests a judgment about what is too much weight; *chubby* suggests cuteness; *stout* suggests sturdiness; and *plump* means "fully rounded, fat in a pleasant way." You may want to use *chubby* or *plump* to suggest that the clown is cute or pleasingly rounded.

Affixes

Choosing the right word will mean choosing between words that look similar but mean different things. For example, what is the difference between *regular* and *irregular* or between *lucky* and *unlucky?* These pairs of words are antonyms that were created by the addition of an affix. An **affix** is a syllable or syllables that are combined with a base word, or root, to make a new word. If the affix comes before the root, it is called a **prefix.** If it comes after the root, it is called a **suffix.**

Dis- is a prefix that turns a word into its opposite. *Honest* becomes *dishonest; trust* becomes *distrust.* The prefixes *ir-* and *un-* also turn the meaning of the word into the opposite of the root. The suffix *-er* refers to a person who does a certain job—as in *writer* and *gardener.* Words with this ending can be useful to you as you revise your writing.

> **Before** My uncle earns his living by writing all kinds of things, such as stories, plays, business reports, and even cookbooks.

> **After** My uncle is a *writer.*

When you revise your writing, check to see that you have not confused two words that have the same root. For example, look at the following words. They are all made by adding a prefix to the word *cycle.*

unicycle   bicycle   tricycle

Which form of the word *cycle* would you use to describe something a circus performer might ride? Which form of the word is correct for a very young child's three-wheeler? If you know that *uni-* means "one," *bi-* means "two," and *tri-* means "three," you won't have to guess which word is correct.

Following is a list of some common prefixes and suffixes and sample words. You can use the list to help you choose the right word.

Prefix	Meaning	Sample Words
a-	on	ashore, afire, atop
anti-	against	antifreeze, antidote, antislavery
auto-	self	autograph, automobile, autobiography
bi-, bin-	two, twice	bicuspid, biceps, binary
co-	with, together	co-worker, coincident, coalition
dec-	ten	decade, decimal, decathlon
dis-	not	dishonest, distrustful, discontent
dis-	opposite	disarrange, discomfort, disconnect
ex-	out	exit, exclude, excerpt
hept-, sept-	seven	heptagon, septennial, septet
il-	not	illegal, illogical, illegible
im-	not	immovable, immobile, immature
in-	not	inactive, incorrect, indefinite
ir-	not	irregular, irrational, irrelevant
kilo-	1,000	kilocycle, kilogram, kilometer
macro-	large, long	macron, macrocosm, macromodel
micro-	small	microscopic, microfilm, microsurgery
milli-	1/1,000	millimeter, milligram, millisecond
mis-	wrong	misspell, misdeed, misbehave
mono-	one	monorail, monotone
poly-	many	polygon, polysyllable, polytheism
post-	after	postscript, postpone, postdate
pre-	before	predict, presume, precede
re-	back	refund, repay, return
re-	again	reread, rearrange, rediscover
semi-	half	semicircle, semiannual, semifinals
sub-	under, below	submarine, subsoil, subnormal
trans-	across, over	transportation, transform, transcontinental
tri-	three	triangle, tricycle, triad
un-	not	unsafe, unsure, unreliable
uni-	one	unit, unicycle, unify

Suffix	Meaning	Sample Words
-able, -ible	can be done	eatable, lovable, readable
-an	relating to	historian, American, European
-ant, -ent	person who	immigrant, assistant, resident
-en	to make	lengthen, shorten, weaken
-er	comparative degree	faster, lighter, clearer
-er, -or	person connected with	lawyer, barber, actor
-ery, -ry	place where	bakery, rookery, laundry
-et, -ette	small	dinette, kitchenette, statuette
-ful	enough to fill	capful, spoonful, mouthful
-ing	material	roofing, bedding, siding
-ion	act, process	construction, rebellion, revolution
-ious	characterized by	gracious, ambitious, infectious
-ish	like, pertaining to	Scottish, clownish, whitish
-ism	doctrine, system	Quakerism, Americanism, realism
-ist	person who	biologist, botanist, socialist
-ity	state of	sincerity, necessity, acidity
-less	without	homeless, doubtless, careless
-let	small	streamlet, leaflet, bracelet
-like	like	homelike, lifelike, apelike
-logy	science of	biology, zoology, psychology
-ly	characteristic of, in the manner of, like	fatherly, motherly, friendly
-ness	state of, quality of, condition of	greatness, kindness, dimness
-oid	like	asteroid, planetoid, humanoid
-or	person who	auditor, donor, creditor
-ory	place where	conservatory, laboratory, lavatory
-ous	having the qualities of	glamorous, joyous, poisonous
-ster	one belonging to, characterized by	gangster, huckster, youngster
-wise	way, manner	clockwise, lengthwise, slantwise

Specific Words

To give your words the power of "lightning," replace a general word with a more specific one. You'll need to think like you did when you narrowed your topic.

☞ **Narrowing Your Topic, page 18.**

Nouns. You create a more vivid picture in your readers' minds when you use more specific nouns. **Nouns** are words that name a person, place, thing, idea, action, or quality.

> **Before** The bird landed in the tree.
>
> **After** The *wren* landed in the *oak*.

Proper nouns name *particular* people, places, or things. They always begin with capital letters. *Congress, the White House, Golden Gate Bridge, Tennessee, Canada,* and *Thomas Jefferson* are all proper nouns. Proper nouns are always more specific than other nouns, called **common nouns.**

> **Before** A young woman spoke up forcefully. "Don't close the beach!" she cried. The police officer looked miserable.
>
> **After** *Ms. Kawalki* spoke up forcefully. "Don't close *Morningside Beach!*" she cried. *Officer Lightfoot* looked miserable.

Common nouns can be abstract or concrete. **Abstract nouns** name things that cannot be touched or seen, such as actions, qualities, or ideas. Using an abstract noun is sometimes the only way to express an idea, but such nouns can be vague. **Concrete nouns** name things that you can see or touch. They add details to your writing that make it convincing and real.

Common Nouns	
Abstract	**Concrete**
honor	rock
feeling	cloud
love	computer

As you revise your draft, ask yourself whether an abstract noun is really necessary. If it is, keep it. If not, replace it with a more concrete noun.

> Before Julio was interested in justice.
>
> After Julio wanted to be a *lawyer*.

Using Unbiased Language. Many common names for jobs, such as *mailman* and *fireman*, end with *-man* or *-men*. Although these jobs can be held by men or women, the words seem to give more importance to men. Often, you can use unbiased words that apply equally to men and women. You will find the following list useful when you are looking over your draft to be sure the language you used is fair to both men and women.

Old Word	New Words
businessman	business person, business leader, merchant
cavemen	early humans, prehistoric people
chairman	chairperson, chair, moderator
fireman	fire fighter
forefathers	ancestors
mailman	letter carrier, mail carrier, postal worker
mankind	humanity, humankind
manpower	work force, personnel, workers
men	humans, people, human beings, persons
policeman	police officer
salesman	salesperson, salesclerk
workman	worker

Pronouns. A **pronoun** is a word that takes the place of a noun by standing for a person or a thing without naming it. *He, she, it, I, we, they, her, everyone, you,* and *them* are examples of pronouns. Such words are very useful when you find you've used a proper noun too many times.

> **Before** When Sylvia took in the mail, Sylvia received a phone call. Then Sylvia and Raul began frantically to pack for their vacation. Sylvia and Raul had a train to catch at noon.

> **After** When Sylvia took in the mail, *she* received a phone call. Then *she* and Raul began frantically to pack for their vacation. *They* had a train to catch at noon.

Pronouns can also be used to replace a common noun, as in this example.

> **Before** The odd-looking man in the yellow jacket took tea at the Alderton Hotel at 4:00. Then the man rose abruptly from his seat. At precisely 4:35, the man disappeared from the room.

> **After** The odd-looking man took tea at the Alderton Hotel at 4:00. Then *he* rose abruptly from his seat. At precisely 4:35, *he* disappeared from the room.

When you use a pronoun, be sure that the person or thing the pronoun refers to is very clear.

> **Before** After Brad phoned Roberto, he was angry.

> **After** After Brad phoned Roberto, Roberto was angry.
> **Or** Brad was angry after he phoned Roberto.

Verbs. To be sure you are using the most specific word possible, you'll also look at the verbs you've chosen. A **verb** is a word that expresses an action or a state of being. Each sentence has at least one verb. An **action verb** expresses a physical or mental action. *Chase, send, wonder, tumble, balance,* and *leap* are all action verbs. Action verbs make your writing come alive. A **state of being verb** expresses a condition or state of being. *Seem, feel, appear, look, become,* and *be* are examples of this kind. These words are general, but you may need to use them at times.

You may find yourself using the same verbs over and over again in your writing. *Is, see, walk, go, talk, say,* and other common verbs are easy to overuse. As with nouns, you can find a more specific verb to replace a general one. Notice the difference the verb choice makes in the following sentences.

Using a
Thesaurus,
page 38.

> Dwayne *walked* to the door and *knocked* on it.
>
> Dwayne *rushed* to the door and *banged* on it.
>
> Dwayne *ambled* to the door and *tapped* on it.

The specific words you choose will depend on the feelings and information you want to express.

Using a Dictionary
You'll often find a dictionary useful when revising your writing. A **dictionary** is a reference book that gives the meanings of words. Usually, the most common definition comes first. Dictionaries also are useful for finding synonyms and antonyms and for finding out how to pronounce words, spell them, and divide them into syllables. Sometimes the words are used in sample sentences. All this information for a word is called a **dictionary entry.**

Dictionary entries appear in alphabetical order. **Guide words** at the tops of the pages show you the first and last entry words on a page (or on two facing pages). You'll know the word you're looking for is on one of those pages if it comes alphabetically between the two guide words. The entry for *November,* for instance, would appear between the guide words *notice* and *novice.*

Sample Dictionary Entry

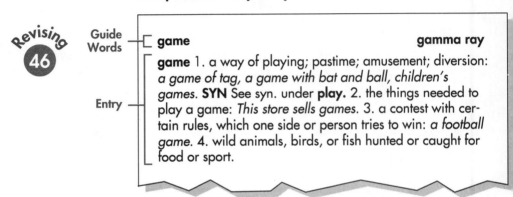

Guide Words

game   **gamma ray**

Entry

game 1. a way of playing; pastime; amusement; diversion: *a game of tag, a game with bat and ball, children's games.* **SYN** See syn. under **play.** 2. the things needed to play a game: *This store sells games.* 3. a contest with certain rules, which one side or person tries to win: *a football game.* 4. wild animals, birds, or fish hunted or caught for food or sport.

You can decide if you are using the right words simply by reading the definitions and any explanations for synonyms. In the sample entry, you would have to look up *play* to find the following synonyms.

—**Syn.** *n.* **1 Play, sport, game** mean activity or exercise of mind or body engaged in for recreation or fun. **Play** is the general word. **Sport** applies to any form of athletics or an outdoor pastime, whether it requires much or little activity or is merely watched. **Game** applies especially to an activity in the form of a contest played by certain rules.

Polishing Style

You've heard of hair styles or fashion styles. Well, your writing should have a style of its own—the way it lets your ideas shine through. Just as combing your hair in a certain way or wearing a belt can change your overall look, so, too, your writing style can be "dressed up" by changing or adding words and sentences.

Sentence Variety

One very noticeable change you can make to improve your writing style is to use a variety of kinds of sentences. A **sentence** is a group of words that expresses a complete thought. Using different sentence structures adds interest and rhythm to your writing. Consider this example:

> **Before** Jerzy came out of the locker room. He climbed the ladder. He stood on the diving board. He dove into the pool.

The sentences sound jerky because they're short and about the same length. They're not interesting to read. You could revise them this way:

> **After** Jerzy came out of the locker room and climbed the ladder. After standing on the diving board a moment, he dove into the pool.

The revision flows better and is more interesting to read. There are many other ways you could revise the sentences to tell the same information. In the following discussion you will see some of the kinds of sentences you can use.

A sentence contains a subject and a predicate. The **subject** is the part of a sentence about which something is said. *Jerzy* and *he* are the subjects of the sample sentences. The **predicate** is the part of the sentence that says something about the subject.

Came out of the locker room is the predicate in the first sentence of the "before" example. The subject usually—but not always—comes first in a sentence. For example, you could write *Into the pool he dove.* Even though it is last, *he* is still the subject.

The **simple subject** is the noun or pronoun about which something is said. The verb that says something about the subject is the **simple predicate**. The **complete subject** is the simple subject plus all words that go with it; the **complete predicate** is the verb and all words that go with it. In the following examples, the simple subject and simple predicate are underlined.

Revising
48

Complete Subject	Complete Predicate
The <u>boy</u> with the least points	finally <u>won</u> a lap.
<u>Jody</u>	<u>jumped</u> into the pool with a giant splash.

Compound subjects are two or more nouns or pronouns that are the subject of one verb. **Compound predicates** are two or more verbs that have the same subject. These are underlined in the following examples.

Complete Subject	Complete Predicate
Always competitive, <u>Jenny</u> and <u>Beth</u>	<u>tied</u> in each event they entered.
The weary <u>coach</u>	<u>mopped</u> her brow and <u>glanced</u> at the sad news on the scoreboard.

In most of your writing you will want to use complete sentences so your ideas are clear to readers. Therefore, when you revise, you'll want to be on the lookout for sentence fragments. A **sentence fragment** is a group of words that doesn't express a complete thought or is missing either a subject or predicate.

> after the moon rose (not a complete thought)
> the waves on the lake (no predicate)
> bucked like broncos (no subject)

To change a fragment into a sentence, you need to ask what it would take to complete the thought. The fragments in the example could be combined into a complete sentence.

> After the moon rose, the waves on the lake bucked like broncos.

Types of Sentences. Remember, you are thinking like your readers when you revise. Readers notice if the rhythm of your sentences is jolting, smooth, or tangled. If every sentence seems to fit the pattern *The (noun) (verb)*, you might put your readers to sleep! Therefore, you want to use a variety of types of sentences. You can choose from among four main types: simple, compound, complex, and compound-complex. Each type uses the basic building blocks—subject and predicate—arranged or combined in several ways.

To understand fully how the four sentence types are built, however, you need to know about another type of building block, or sentence part, called a **clause**. A **clause** is a group of related words that contains a subject and a predicate. If it expresses a complete thought, it is called an **independent clause.** As its name states, an independent clause can stand alone as a sentence. A **dependent clause** is one that does not express a complete idea and cannot stand by itself. Dependent clauses are sentence fragments like the following examples:

> where the road curves sharply left
> that Ms. Ramirez built last year
> when the door opens
> whoever gets there first

Although dependent clauses have nouns and verbs, they must be attached to an independent clause to form a sentence.

The sentences you saw in the complete subject and complete predicate charts are simple sentences —the first type of sentence. A **simple sentence** is made of one independent clause. This is the most common sentence form. You're likely to find you've used simple sentences quite often in your writing. A simple sentence can have a compound subject, a compound predicate, or both.

The second type of sentence is built by combining two simple sentences. A **compound sentence** contains two or more independent clauses. The two clauses may be joined by a comma along with words such as *and, but, for, or, nor, yet,* and *so.* The joining words are called **coordinating conjunctions.**

☞ Checking Usage, page 73.

```
      ┌─── independent clause ───┐   ┌─── independent clause ───┐
```
Tammie furnished the nails, and *Beth supplied the hammers.*

A **complex sentence** contains one independent clause and one or more dependent clauses. You make this kind of sentence when you add a dependent clause to a simple sentence. For example, if you have many short, choppy simple sentences, you might turn one or more into clauses and add them to another sentence. The dependent clauses are underlined in the following "after" example.

Revising
50

Before We watched the clouds. The clouds had brought the rain. The clouds disappeared.

After <u>While we watched,</u> the clouds <u>that had brought the rain</u> disappeared.

The fourth kind of sentence is a combination of a compound and a complex sentence. **Compound-complex sentences** contain two or more independent clauses and one or more dependent clauses. You probably won't use this type of sentence very often. It can be useful, however, if you have several related ideas to express together.

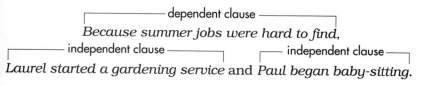

Is a longer sentence a better sentence? Not always. If you add too many dependent clauses to a sentence, the readers may lose sight of the true subject. Sometimes you can improve a sentence by making it into two or more shorter sentences.

Sentence Purposes. Sentences also can be grouped by what they do. Think about the purposes of the following sentences:

> Which state has the most land? The answer is Alaska. Look it up in an encyclopedia. It's more than twice the size of the second largest state, Texas!

The purpose of the first sentence is to ask a question. It is an **interrogative sentence.** The second sentence, called a **declarative sentence,** states a fact (or an opinion). The third sentence is an **imperative sentence**—it gives a command or makes a request. The subject of an imperative sentence is the word *you*, which is not stated but is understood. The last sentence is **exclamatory**—it expresses a strong feeling .

Declarative sentences are the most common. If you're giving directions, you'll probably use a lot of imperative sentences. However, you can add variety to your writing by adding a few interrogative or exclamatory sentences.

> **Before** I wasn't sure she was coming. I kept looking down the hall for her.

> **After** Was she coming? I kept looking down the hall for her.

Elaboration

Elaborating, or adding details to your writing, allows you to present a more complete picture. For example, once two young neighbors who wanted to make money set up car washes across the street from each other. The competition heated up, and as you can see in the picture, their advertising signs reflected it. You, too, can add details to your writing. The following pages tell about different kinds of words you can use to elaborate on your subject.

Adjectives. An **adjective** describes a quality or condition of a noun. What do you picture as you read each of these adjectives with the word *city?*

> lonely city, familiar city, exciting city,
> crowded city, distant city, beautiful city

You can use several adjectives in a row for a stronger effect.

> Theresa was *nervous* and *exhausted* by the time of the tryouts.

> *Cold, dark,* and *empty,* the cave awaited exploration.

Adjectives are especially useful in narrative or descriptive writing when you want to create a clear picture in readers' eyes. Without the adjectives, the following paragraph would seem less real and specific.

> Helen climbed over the *old stone* fence into the *overgrown* garden. Rows of *bright* flowers bloomed among the *spreading* weeds. She still could make out the *well-worn* paths among the flower beds. The *marble* fountain was dry.

To get the most out of adjectives, choose them carefully. You should be able to think of a good reason for each one you use. Some adjectives may be unnecessary or may repeat details that have already been stated, as in the following examples:

> We slipped along on the *cold,* icy sidewalk. (If it's icy, it has to be cold.)

> The large, giant ape eyed the zoo visitors. (*Large* and *giant* are synonyms.)

With adjectives—as with nouns and verbs—the more specific, the better. Avoid general adjectives such as *nice, good, old,* and *small.* Look for adjectives that are more specific, for example, *kind, thoughtful, ancient,* and *acorn-sized.*

Adverbs. Another type of word that adds description is an **adverb.** These words **modify**, or tell more about, verbs, adjectives, or other adverbs. How would the picture in the reader's mind change with each of these combinations of the verb *walked* and an adverb?

> walked lazily, walked swiftly, walked clumsily, walked stiffly, walked cautiously, walked feebly

Adverbs answer the questions "How?" "When?" "Where?" or "To what extent?" In fact, the words *how, why, when,* and *where* are themselves adverbs.

How?	Sylvie ate an apple *eagerly.*
When?	She'll have another one *later.*
Where?	She got it over *there.*
To what extent?	She ate *almost* all of them.

When you read your draft, examine the words surrounding the verbs. Do they help you get across your ideas? For example, if you're describing a laboratory procedure, you might add adverbs to make the description more precise.

> **Before** Set the beaker of liquid on the table. Then add the solid pellets to the liquid. Stir the mixture.

> **After** *Gently* set the beaker of liquid on the table. Then, *gradually* add the solid pellets to the liquid. Stir the mixture *carefully.*

Prepositions. Perhaps without even being aware of it, you often elaborate sentences by using prepositions and prepositional phrases. A **preposition** is a word or group of words that shows a relationship to some other word in a sentence.

Prepositions				
about	because of	between	in spite of	to
above	before	by	of	toward
across	behind	down	off	under
after	below	for	on	until
around	beneath	from	out	up
at	beside	in	over	with

A **phrase** is a group of related words that doesn't have a subject and a predicate. When a phrase contains a preposition, it is called a **prepositional phrase.** Sometimes you can improve your sentences by elaborating with prepositional phrases.

> Before The molten lava spread.
> After *During the eruption,* the molten lava spread *across the valley.*

Figures of Speech. When you write to explain or describe, you can often make your point clearer by adding comparisons. **Figures of speech** are imaginative ways of describing or comparing two different things or actions. Imagination plays a big role in writing figures of speech because you help the reader look at something in a new way.

Three kinds of figures of speech you might use are similes, metaphors, and analogies. A **simile** is a comparison using *like* or *as*. It shows how two unlike objects have something in common.

> Hail fell *like Ping-Pong balls* from the sky.

A **metaphor** is a comparison made without using *like* or *as*. With it an object is given the characteristics of another.

> The cat *was a Ping-Pong ball* bouncing after the mouse.

An **analogy** is an extended comparison in which more than one point is compared.

> The game was a *battle* between evenly matched sides. *Like brave soldiers*, the players massed on either side of the field. At a signal from the *chief commanding officers*, the teams charged toward their opponents—*enemies for the afternoon.*

Transitions

You've looked at individual words and sentences. Now step back a bit and look at how the sentences and paragraphs relate to each other. Pay attention to the order of the various paragraphs. Would another arrangement work better? Are all the paragraphs on the same idea in the same place? Do they seem connected to make a smooth whole? If not, see if you can add transitions such as those in the following list. **Transitions** link a sentence or paragraph to what has immediately preceded it. Use them near the beginning of a new sentence or paragraph to alert your readers to a turn in thought.

Transitions

first	second	next	before	now
then	afterward	to sum up	as a result	on the other hand
while	because	during	so	in conclusion
to this point	nevertheless	hence	however	moreover
otherwise	therefore	still	thus	

The words you use for a transition will depend on the type of writing and the relationships of ideas. However, if the transition doesn't sound natural to you, don't use it. You don't want your writing style to sound stuffy or as if you're showing off.

Tone

Two important parts of planning your writing were deciding why you were writing and who would be reading it. Your answers led you to write in a certain tone—formal or informal. Following are two examples of tone. Which one was written for a class assignment? The other one was written to explain a procedure to a group of friends.

Why Are You Writing?, pages 9–12.

> Carefully peel back the bark of the tree in a small area. With a pair of tweezers, gently lift an insect into the specimen jar. Next, clearly label the jar with the time, location, and name of the species. Then replace the bark.

> Here's how you get your bugs. First, lift a small flap of bark. Be careful not to hurt the tree! Then try to grab one of the creatures with your tweezers. Pop the bug in the jar and label it with who, what, where, and when. Don't forget to close the bark.

Read through your draft to see if your tone is the same from beginning to end. Consider how your changes in content, wording, and style mesh. Does the draft sound natural and flow smoothly? How do you think readers will respond to it?

Revision Checklist

The Revision Checklist is a guide to revising. Only *you* can decide which of the items you need to do. Make sure you are happy with your changes so that your readers will be pleased, too.

Will readers understand the information?
- ❑ explain terms
- ❑ add needed information
- ❑ remove extra information
- ❑ rearrange order

Did I use "lightning" words?
- ❑ include synonyms or antonyms with the right connotation
- ❑ correct the affixes
- ❑ use specific nouns and verbs
- ❑ check for unbiased language
- ❑ use pronouns

Is the style polished so my ideas shine through?
- ❑ vary sentence types and lengths
- ❑ elaborate with adjectives, adverbs, prepositions, and figures of speech
- ❑ include transitions
- ❑ check tone

CHAPTER FOUR

EDITING

Before sharing your writing with others, you have one last step to complete—editing. **Editing** is the "business" part of writing in which you correct errors in spelling and use of words, capital letters, and punctuation marks. This step gets your work ready for a wider audience.

When you edit, you ask yourself questions such as these:

○ Have I spelled the words correctly?

○ Have I consistently told my story, using the past, present, or future tense where it is needed?

○ Have I used capital letters where they are needed?

○ Are the commas, periods, and other punctuation marks in place?

When you are finished, you want your writing to be like a clear window, so that your ideas or story can shine through. When you can answer yes to all these questions, there are no longer any smudges on the glass.

Suppose you've written this journal entry:

Yesterday I had hi hopes for our band the motions. today none. I'm hopeless. Without a lot more mony we wont get off the ground to fly to state. And that to bad cause were awesome.

Then you get the idea of writing your Uncle Zack to see if he can help you with money-raising ideas for the band. You want to tell him the same things that you wrote in your journal, but you want to say them properly. You don't want him to be distracted by odd words

or spellings, so you edit your work and come up
with this version:

> Yesterday I had <u>high</u> hopes for our band,
> the <u>Motions</u>. <u>Today</u> <u>I</u> <u>have</u> none. <u>I</u> <u>feel</u> hope-
> less. Without a lot more <u>money,</u> we won<u>'</u>t
> get off the ground to fly to <u>the</u> state <u>contest</u>.
> That<u>'</u>s <u>too</u> bad<u>,</u> <u>because</u> we<u>'</u>re awesome.

You have found and corrected misspelled words,
incomplete sentences, and errors in capitalization
and punctuation. Although you haven't changed
your ideas at all, Uncle Zack is more likely to
understand them. Which version do you think
Uncle Zack will respond better to? Why? By
answering why, you can see for yourself the importance of editing. *Not* editing your writing is like
going to a fancy party in wrinkled clothes.

✔Checking Spelling

Some schools require only that you dress neatly.
You can choose which clothes you wear. Other
schools require uniforms. You must wear only
the shirt and the pants or skirt that came with
the uniform. Spelling is like going to a school
where uniforms are required.

Just as there are many different combinations
of clothes you could wear if you were allowed,
there are many combinations of letters that could
be used to spell different sounds. Look at the different spellings of the *sh* sound in these words:

di**sh**wa**sh**er   ma**ch**ine   spe**ci**al   na**ti**on

However, there is usually only one way to spell a
word correctly. For example, long ago it was decided that *nice* would be spelled *nice,* not *nyce, nyse,*
or *nise.* A first step to correct spelling is knowing
how English sounds *can* be spelled. The following
list will help.

Common Spellings of English Sounds

a	ask, plaid, calf, laugh
ā	age, rain, straight, gauge, may, café, break, vein, eight, crochet, hey
ah	father, palm, sergeant, hearth
ãr	air, aerial, prayer, tear, their, heir
aw	all, Utah, balk, cause, law, recording, broad, four, sought
b	bat, rubber
ch	cello, check, Czech, witch, righteous, question, structure
d	do, add, skilled
e	many, said, lend, thread, heifer, leopard, friend, bury
ē	algae, ecology, lean, tree, receive, key, ski, grief, actually
f	for, stiff, cough, calf, phone
g	goat, beggar, ghost, guess, vague
h	hat, who
hw	when
i	elect, it, carriage, sieve, women, busy, guild, myth
ī	aisle, kayak, height, geyser, ice, pie, thigh, coyote, guide, guy, my
j	graduate, midget, soldier, gem, exaggerate, region, jump
k	cat, accuse, school, stack, acquit, king, khaki, talk, antique
l	like, stall
m	palm, mine, comb, summer, hymn
n	gnarled, knight, nice, dinner, pneumonia
ng	link, handkerchief, strong, tongue
o	watch, honor, nod, knowledge

Common Spellings of English Sounds

ō	chauffeur, plateau, sew, cold, roach, **oh**, brooch, soul, dough, grow, owe
oi	boil, toy
oo	wolf, took, would, full
ou	hour, about, bough, gown
p	piece, copper
r	ran, rhyme, marry, write
s	cent, hence, psalm, saw, science, bliss, listen, sword
sh	ocean, chef, vicious, sure, schwa, conscience, shy, pension, tissue, fiction
t	doubt, deceased, receipt, take, thyme, clutter, two
th	thirst
<u>th</u>	this, bathe
u	other, does, blood, young, utter
ū	maneuver, blew, lieutenant, move, shoe, mood, group, through, rude, glue, suit
ur	yearn, ermine, herb, girl, colonel, worst, journal, burn, myrtle
v	of, vase
w	choir, quote, want
y	onion, piñata, yet
yu	beauty, feud, view, unite, cue, youth, yule
z	was, raspberry, scissors, xylophone, zoo, muzzle
zh	mirage, pleasure, vision
ə	about, mountain, authority, effect, dungeon, purity, parliament, offend, porpoise, precious, focus, oxygen

Spelling Rules

Spelling may seem like a mystery, but spelling rules are clues that can help you solve the mystery. They tell you how a word *might* be spelled. Once you know how it might be spelled, you can write it down and see if it looks right. If you aren't sure, you can look up the word in a dictionary.

 Spelling with a Dictionary, page 68.

The following list shows some useful spelling rules. Notice the words that don't follow the rules. You have to remember how those exceptions are spelled.

 Editing 64

Spelling Rules to Remember

Words Like These	Are Usually Spelled This Way	But Not Always
Words with *i*'s and *e*'s: *believe, deceit*	Use *i* before *e* except after *c*, or when sounded like *a* as in *neighbor* and *weigh*. (In those words, use *ei*.)	*ancient, financier; counterfeit, either, foreign, height, leisure, seize, weird*
Words ending in *ede: precede*	The root *cede* is always spelled this way except in four words and their various forms.	*supersede, exceed, proceed, succeed* (and their other forms, such as *superseded, exceeding, proceeds, succeeded*)
Words ending in *c: picnic*	Insert *k* when adding an ending that begins with *e, i,* or *y: picnicked.*	*arced*
Words ending in soft *ce* or *ge: peace, advantage*	Retain the final *e* before adding *-able* or *-ous: peaceable, advantageous.*	

Spelling Rules to Remember

Words Like These	Are Usually Spelled This Way	But Not Always
Words ending in silent e: *love*	Retain the final *e* before suffixes beginning with a consonant: *lovely*.	*argument, duty, truly, judgment, ninth, wholly*
Words ending in silent e: *desire*	Drop the final *e* before suffixes beginning with a vowel: *desirable*.	*mileage, noticeable*
Words ending in ie: *tie*	Change *ie* to *y* when adding *-ing*: *tying*.	
Words ending in oe: *hoe*	Retain the final *e* before a suffix beginning with any vowel **except** *e*: *hoeing* but *hoed*.	
Words ending in *y* preceded by a consonant: *occupy*	Change *y* to *i* before a suffix unless the suffix begins with *i*: *occupies* **but** *occupying*.	
Words of one syllable ending in a consonant preceded by a vowel, and words accented on the last syllable: *glad, repel, occur*	Double the consonant before a suffix beginning with a vowel: *gladden, repelled, occurred*.	*crocheting, ricocheted, filleted, transferable* (**but** *transferred*) Also, if the accent shifts to the first syllable when a suffix is added, the final consonant is not doubled: *preferred* but *preference*.
Words ending in a consonant preceded by more than one vowel: *boil, reveal*	Do not double the consonant before a suffix beginning with a vowel: *boiled, revealing*.	

Spelling Rules to Remember

Editing
66

Words Like These	Are Usually Spelled This Way	But Not Always
Words ending in more than one consonant: *work, conform*	Do not double the final consonant: *worked, conforming.*	
Words not accented on the last syllable: *benefit*	Do not double the final consonant: *benefited.*	
Words ending in *l*: *horizontal*	Retain the *l* before a suffix beginning with *l*: *horizontally.*	Words ending in *ll* drop one *l* before the suffix *ly*: *hilly, fully*
Prefixes *dis-, il- im-, in-, mis-, over-, re-, un-*	Do not change the spelling of the root word: *dissimilar, illegal, immoral, innumerable, misspell, overrun, redo, unnerve.*	
Words ending in a double consonant: *possess, enroll*	Retain both consonants when adding suffixes: *possessor, enrolling.*	
Nouns ending in *f* or *fe*: *handkerchief*	Form the plural by adding *s*: *handkerchiefs*, or by changing the *f* or *fe* to *ve* and adding *s*: *knives, elves, halves, leaves, wives.*	
Nouns ending in *y* preceded by a consonant: *lady*	Form the plural by changing *y* to *i* and adding *es*: *ladies.*	Proper nouns ending in *y* form the plural by adding *s*: "There are three *Garys* in my class."

Spelling Rules to Remember

Words Like These	Are Usually Spelled This Way	But Not Always
Nouns ending in *ch, sh, s, x, z*: *church, brush, glass, gas, fox, topaz*	Form the plural by adding *es*: *churches, brushes, gasses, glasses, foxes, topazes.*	
Nouns ending in *o* preceded by a vowel: *cameo*	Form the plural by adding *s*: *cameos.*	
Nouns ending in *o* preceded by a consonant: *potato*	Form the plural by adding *es*: *potatoes.*	*dittos, dynamos, pianos, silos.* For some nouns, either *s* or *es* is correct: *buffalos* or *buffaloes, volcanos* or *volcanoes.*
Compound nouns: *major general, notary public, sister-in-law*	Make the modified word plural: *major generals, notaries public, sisters-in-law.*	
Nouns ending in *-ful*: *cupful*	Form the plural by adding *s* to *ful*: *cupfuls.*	
Letters, numbers, dates, signs, and words referred to as words	Form the plural by adding *'s*: six *b's*, two *5's*, the *1970's*, *%'s*, *but's.*	

Spelling with a Dictionary

You can use a dictionary to find the correct spelling of any word. To look up a word, you need to know how it *might* be spelled. The word *beautiful*, for example, might be spelled *butiful, beutiful,* or *byutiful*. You don't need to know all of the word to look it up—just the beginning.

☞ **Common Spellings of English Words, pages 62–63.**

First look in the dictionary under the spelling you think is most likely. Perhaps you choose to begin with *bu-*. If you don't find *beautiful* there, you might recall there is an *e* in the word and look up *beu-*. Looking at the nearby entries—above and below—you will probably find the correct spelling.

If you still can't find a word, try looking up a synonym. In the entry for *handsome*, for example, you will find "**SYN** see *beautiful*."

Homophones

Words that sound the same but are spelled differently and have different meanings are called **homophones.**

> No talking *allowed*. (*No talking is permitted.*)
>
> No talking *aloud*. (*You may talk in a whisper.*)
>
> She had a good *role* in the play. (*She played a good part.*)
>
> She had a good *roll* for her sandwich. (*She ate a small bread that tasted good.*)

There are many homophone pairs—and even sets of three or four homophones. People sometimes use one spelling for another by mistake. (Even computer spell-checking programs miss places where the wrong homonym is used.) The following examples will help you check some homophones.

Words That Sound Alike

Homophones in Sentences	Homophone Meanings
She gave the soldier first *aid*.	assistance, help
He left a message with the general's *aide*.	assistant, helper
The *air* smells sweet.	gases surrounding the earth
The *heir* cannot be found.	one who has the right to another's property after the owner dies
The candles were on the *altar*.	table used in religious worship
This will not *alter* our plans.	change
Her *ant* farm is flourishing.	small insect
Cher's *aunt* is visiting.	sister or sister-in-law of one's mother or father
We watched the balloon's *ascent*.	upward movement
Jeb gave his *assent*.	approval, agreement
Jilly *ate* many pretzels.	chewed and swallowed
After *eight* she felt ill.	the number 8
The trees were *bare*.	uncovered
We could see the black *bear*.	large animal
She *beat* the drum slowly.	hit, struck
Nell pulled up a giant *beet*.	red vegetable
He's *been* gone one week.	past form of *be*
The coal *bin* was nearly empty.	container
The wind *blew* fiercely.	past form of *blow*
Their faces turned *blue*.	color
The *board* split neatly in two.	piece of wood
The fans were *bored*.	weary and restless
Lowell was a shy *boy*.	young man
The sailboat rounded the *buoy*.	marker in the water
The left *brake* failed.	device for stopping
We need a *break*.	intermission
Buy me a treat!	purchase
Jesse sat *by* the train window.	beside, next to
Begin each sentence with a *capital* letter.	large letter, such as *A, B*
He worked in the *Capitol* building.	where state or national legislature meets

Editing
69

Words That Sound Alike

Homophones in Sentences	Homophone Meanings
Sue patched the flaking *ceiling*. Tom closed the letter with *sealing* wax.	surface overhead used to seal shut
The *cellar* is damp and dark. The *seller* is clever and quick.	underground room one who sells
He forgot to *close* the trunk. He wore old *clothes* for the job.	shut, lock, seal garments
The river took a winding *course*. The sand on its banks was *coarse*.	path, direction made of large parts; not fine
The stunt was a great *feat*. She landed on her *feet*.	show of great skill or daring more than one foot
From grain they made *flour*. He bought a white *flower*.	finely ground meal blossom
The key fell through the *grate*. The woman is a *great* poet.	framework of bars famous
It made a low *groan*. He found a *grown* possum.	deep moan full-sized
She *guessed* he was happy. He had been a perfect *guest*.	supposed, thought visitor
The *hail* beat on the roof. He was a *hale* ninety-year-old.	frozen rain healthy
He *heard* a loud roar. The *herd* charged the corral.	took in sounds through the ear group of animals of one kind
I can *hear* them now. *Here* they are!	take in sounds through the ear in this place
You *know* it's true. They have *no* sense!	understand not any
The swelling will *lessen*. You've learned a *lesson*.	shrink instructive experience
I got it through the *mail*. It was a *male* pig.	postal service the same gender as a man or boy
He stated the *main* idea clearly. The horse's *mane* was thick.	most important long heavy hair on the back of the neck
He works at the *mall*. The lion could *maul* the cub.	large shopping center beat and pull about

Words That Sound Alike

Homophones in Sentences	Homophone Meanings
The scouts will grill the *meat*.	flesh from animals
They *meet* on Tuesdays.	get together
Leaders will *mete* out supplies.	give a share of
Only *one* team can win.	a single
It's too bad they *won*.	had a victory
The *pail* sprang a leak.	bucket
The yellow paint was very *pale*.	without much color
They needed *patience*.	willingness to put up with waiting
The *patients* had to wait.	people being treated by a doctor
The dress was *plain* but pretty.	simple, undecorated
Use a *plane* to smooth the wood.	hand tool
Our *principal* smiles a lot.	head of a school
She has one guiding *principle*.	basic truth or belief
It's time to *raise* the flag.	put up
It gave off brilliant *rays*.	beams of light
They plan to *raze* the shack.	tear down
He heard a sharp *rap* on the door.	quick, light blow
You need to *wrap* the package.	cover
The *road* was bumpy and uneven.	route, street
They *rode* their bikes.	sat on something and made it go
She *rowed* across the lake.	used oars to move a boat
We saw the balloon *sail* over the treetops.	cruise
This car is for *sale*.	available for purchase
Tracy will *sew* new curtains.	make by stitching
He said things that were not *so*.	true
It's time to *sow* the rye seed.	plant by scattering
Snakes will *steal* eggs.	take wrongfully
The beams were solid *steel*.	hard metal
Their dinner is about ready.	belonging to them
The class is over *there*.	at that place
I hope *they're* ready to eat.	they are
I drove her *to* the pool.	toward
I work there, *too*.	also
She has *two* jobs.	the number 2

Editing

71

Your Spelling Memory

Many writers stumble over the words on the following list. Which ones trip you up? Study those words and check your writing for your personal spelling stumbling blocks. After a while you will remember these words and how they are spelled.

Words That Are Often Misspelled

absence	desperate	lightning	resistance
acceptance	disappear	likely	resource
accidentally	disease	literature	restaurant
ache	doctor	mathematics	rhythm
achievement	eighth	medicine	ridiculous
acquaintance	embarrass	minute	roommate
acquire	envelop	muscle	scarcely
across	envelope	mystery	schedule
advice	environment	necessary	scissors
all right	excellent	niece	sentence
already	exercise	night .	separate
angle	existence	ninety	skiing
answer	expense	noisily	strength
apparent	experience	noticeable	sugar
appropriate	extraordinary	occasionally	synonym
approximately	familiar	occurrence	temporary
assistant	fascinating	often	therefore
awkward	forty	operate	thorough
because	friend	ordinarily	tomorrow
bicycle	genius	original	truly
bulletin	governor	pastime	typical
business	guess	peculiar	twelfth
captain	happening	picnicking	until
career	height	pleasant	vacuum
ceiling	history	possibility	vague
characteristic	huge	preparation	variety
chocolate	immediately	procedure	vegetable
coming	impossible	pursue	wear
commercial	incidentally	quiet	whether
confidence	independent	quite	won't
control	inevitable	raise	would
convenience	innocent	realize	writer
debt	interfere	receive	written
definite	knowledge	recognize	wrote
description	laboratory	repeat	yield

Checking Usage

If you play in an orchestra or band, you want to play in harmony with the others. You don't want to squawk when you should warble. **Usage** defines the rules for playing in harmony in the world of language. When you think about the function different words have in a sentence, it helps to know the **parts of speech.**

The Eight Parts of Speech

Part of Speech	Role in Sentence	Examples
Nouns	Name a person, place, thing, idea, action, or quality	player, conductor, flute, bandstand, harmony, march
Pronouns	Stand for people without naming them	I, you, he, she, it, we, they
Adjectives	Tell about a noun or a pronoun	fast, high, low, sour, peaceful
Verbs	Express an action or state-of-being	play, strike, march, step, dance
Adverbs	Tell about a verb, adjective, or adverb	slowly, quickly, there, very
Prepositions	Show the relationship of a noun or pronoun to another word	about, behind, on, to, toward, under, up, with
Conjunctions	Join words, phrases, clauses, or sentences	and, but, or, for, nor, yet, so
Interjections	Express an emotion	bravo, hooray, ouch, oops, oh

Notice that some words can be more than one part of speech. The role a word plays in a sentence determines its part of speech.

Verb The band will *march* in two rows.
Noun We played a *march* composed by Sousa.

Agreement

Some parts of a sentence must match or **agree**. You can think of this agreement as a handshake to seal

a promise. If the two hands miss each other—if the two parts that should go together don't—the agreement is not complete.

Subject/Verb Agreement. The subject and verb of a sentence must agree. Usually this agreement is a matter of **number.** *Singular* means "one"; *plural* means "more than one." If you have a singular subject (such as *Rosie, a bat,* or *a baseball*), you must choose the singular verb (such as *goes, hits,* or *is*).

Janis *grabs* her mitt and *leaves* the house.

Agreement can be tricky when the subject and verb are farther apart:

Jason, one of our best fielders, *plays* third base.

☞ **Sentence Variety, pages 47–49.** If the subject is compound and connected by *and* (such as *Rosie and I*) or if it is plural (*bats*), you must choose the plural form of the verb (*go, hit,* or *are*).

Janis and LeRoy *grab* their mitts and *leave* the house.

If you have two singular subjects connected by *or,* use the verb you would use for one:

> When the ball comes their way,
> either Jeb or Maria *catches* it.

If the verb comes before the subject, the two still must agree:

> Along the baseline *flies* the foul ball.

When a pronoun is the subject of a sentence, it must agree with the verb. Pronouns such as *anyone, each, either, neither, everybody, everyone, nobody,* and *someone* are treated as singular subjects.

> Everyone *attacks* the umpire at once.

Indefinite pronouns such as *both, few, many,* and *several* take plural forms of the verb.

> Both of them *are* talented pitchers.

Pronoun/Antecedent Agreement. A pronoun must agree with the word it stands for—its **antecedent.** The pronoun and antecedent must have the same number (singular or plural) and **gender** (male, female, or neutral).

> Jason and Gabe brought all *their* bats.
> Sharon brought *her* batting helmet.

Some pronouns can be either singular or plural depending on their antecedents. *All, any, most, none,* and *some* are these changeable pronouns.

$$\text{Most of the fans were yelling.}$$

$$\text{Most of the field was muddy.}$$

Pronouns must have clear antecedents.

> **Before** Before Ted and Latisha got the cooler to the ballpark, it fell apart.

It is not clear what fell apart—the ballpark or the cooler.

> **After** The cooler fell apart before Ted and Latisha got it to the ballpark.

Sudden Changes in Direction

As much as possible, stay on the same course in writing. If you begin telling a story in the past, continue in the past.

☞ **Tense, pages 82–83.**

> **Before** We wanted to go to Circus City. We think about it every day. We plan to go during vacation.
>
> **After** We wanted to go to Circus City. We *thought* about it every day. We *planned* to go during vacation.

If you begin writing using *I, me,* or *my*—called writing in the first person—stay with that approach.

> *I* dreamed of riding the giant Ferris wheel. It was *my* favorite ride.

If you begin a sentence with a plural subject, continue using the plural subject and the plural form of the verb.

> **Before** Trips to the amusement park are nice, but *it takes* a lot of planning.
>
> **After** Trips to the amusement park are nice, but *they take* a lot of planning.

Sentence Faults

Incomplete sentences, or fragments, can usually be combined with whole sentences to make them complete.

Sentence Variety, pages 47–51.

> **Before** The giant roller coaster. I almost backed out.
>
> **After** *When I saw* the giant roller coaster, I almost backed out.

You may find some **run-on sentences.** These are two or more sentences run together. Sometimes the independent clauses are separated only by a comma. At other times they aren't separated at all. The following examples show four ways to correct run-on sentences.

Editing
77

> **Before** Our car for the water ride went under a waterfall, I got the drenching of my life!
>
> **After** Our car for the water ride went under a waterfall. I got the drenching of my life! *(Make two separate sentences.)*

> **Or** Our car for the water ride went under a waterfall; I got the drenching of my life! *(Use a semicolon between the clauses.)*

> **Or** Our car for the water ride went under a waterfall, and I got the drenching of my life! *(Use a comma and a conjunction between the clauses.)*

> **Or** When our car for the water ride went under a waterfall, I got the drenching of my life! *(Make one part into a phrase or a subordinate clause.)*

Parallel Expressions

If you have ever been skiing, you know the skier has to keep both skis facing the same way—or **parallel.** Certain parts of sentences should be parallel as well. Ideas that are similar—like items in a list—should be written in the same way.

> **Before** Skiing, to swim, and tennis are my favorite activities.
>
> **After** Skiing, *swimming,* and *playing* tennis are my favorite activities.

It is important to make phrases and verb forms parallel as well.

> **Before** On the court and poolside, I get good exercise.
>
> **After** On the court and *in the pool,* I get good exercise.
>
> **Before** Having learned the sport and after getting good at it, I began to relax.
>
> **After** Having learned the sport and *having gotten* good at it, I began to relax.
>
> **Before** I go to the gym twice a week and am using the rowing machine.
>
> **After** I go to the gym twice a week and *use* the rowing machine.

Problem Modifiers

Misplacing a modifier is like hitting a foul ball in baseball. Although you made contact with the ball, it didn't go where you intended to send it. A misplaced modifier may lead readers in the wrong direction. Modifiers must be carefully placed to make their meaning clear.

Dangling Modifiers. Sometimes modifiers are not connected to any word in the sentence.

> **Before** *Running to catch the train,* the whistle blew.

The whistle isn't running. You need to tell *who* is running.

> **After** *As Alec ran to catch the train,* the whistle blew.
> **Or** *Running to catch the train, Alec* heard the whistle blow.

Squinting Modifiers. An adverb may have been placed between two verbs—both of which it could modify.

> **Before** The train that Alec was running toward frantically sped away.

Was Alec frantically running or was the train frantically speeding?

> **After** The train that Alec was *frantically* running toward sped away.

Misplaced Modifiers. Some modifiers are placed too close to words they are not meant to modify.

> **Before** The woman spoke to the conductor *with a loud voice.*
> **After** The woman *with a loud voice* spoke to the conductor.

The Right Pronoun Form

Just as you wear different clothes for different events, writers use different forms of pronouns for different roles in a sentence. Pronouns that can be used as the subject of a sentence include *I, we, you, he, she, it, they, who,* and *whoever.*

> *I* joined the debate team.
> *She* was already on it.
> *Who* will be the captain?

Nouns or pronouns that receive the action of a verb are called the **direct objects** of the verb. Pronouns that can be used as direct objects include *me, us, you, him, her, it, them, whom,* and *whomever.*

> The podium was heavy. Liza and Sam moved *it* into place.

The same pronouns can be used as **indirect objects.** This means they refer to the person or thing *to whom* or *for whom* the action of the verb is performed.

> Lee gave *me* her notes.

Editing
80

If you use two or more pronouns together, you need to use the correct forms of each of them.

> **Before** Her and I tried out our arguments.
> **After** *She* and I tried out our arguments.
>
> **Before** Paul gave the signal to she and I.
> **After** Paul gave the signal to *her* and *me.*

Good Use of Adjectives

☞ **Elaboration, pages 52–54.**

When you revised your draft, you may have added adjectives to describe people, places, or things more completely. During editing, you'll want to see if you used the adjectives correctly.

Placement of Adjectives. Adjectives often come just before the noun or pronoun they modify. They can be placed after the noun to make a sentence more interesting.

> The actor tripped over the *rusty* bucket backstage.

> Hal, *pale* and *shaken,* made his entrance on cue.

Strong! Stronger!! STRONGEST!!!

Comparison of Adjectives. An advertisement for adjectives might boast, "They come in three strengths—strong, stronger, and strongest." If you are describing a person or thing, you use the **positive** (strong) form. If you are comparing, two people or things, you use the **comparative** (stronger) form. If you want to single out one person or thing among three or more, you use the **superlative** (strongest) form.

Positive	Comparative	Superlative
kind	kinder	kindest
silly	sillier	silliest
talented	more talented	most talented
thoughtful	more thoughtful	most thoughtful
good	better	best
little	less	least

Adjectives of one or sometimes two syllables add -er to form the comparative and -est to form the superlative. Longer adjectives use the words *more* and *most*. Some adjectives, like *good*, are irregular and don't follow either pattern.

☞ **Verbs, page 45.**

Adjectives after Linking Verbs.

Linking verbs include all the forms of *to be* (*am, are, is, was, were*) and the **state-of-being verbs** (*appear, feel, grow, look, seem, smell, sound,* and *taste*). If you want to follow a linking verb with a descriptive word, that word should be an adjective.

> Sylvia is *funny.* Phil is *dramatic.*

Good Use of Verbs

When you revised, perhaps you added more specific verbs to liven up your writing. In addition, you should edit your verb use to make sure it reads smoothly.

Active and Passive Voice. Many verbs can be used in two ways. In the **active voice,** the subject of the verb performs the action. In the **passive voice,** the subject receives the action. Try to use active voice much of the time.

> **Active** My dog *retrieved* the newspaper.
>
> **Passive** The newspaper *was retrieved* by my dog.

Tense. A verb carries with it a sense of time. That time is the verb's **tense.** The three main tenses are past, present, and future. Present tense shows that something is happening now, is a fact, or is a habit. Past tense shows that something already has happened. Future tense shows that something will happen sometime in the future.

> **Past** Kelly *trained* for the Olympics.
>
> **Present** She *swims* the 100-meter freestyle in 59 seconds.
>
> **Future** She *will win* the competition.

Some verbs form their past tense in a predictable way, by ending in -*ed*. Other verbs are **irregular,** or not predictable.

	Present	Past
Regular	follow	followed
	tease	teased
Irregular	be	was
	begin	began
	bring	brought
	buy	bought
	come	came
	do	did
	draw	drew
	eat	ate
	get	got
	hold	held
	lose	lost
	make	made
	ride	rode
	say	said
	take	took
	teach	taught
	write	wrote

Editing
83

You can always find the past tense form of an irregular verb by looking in the dictionary entry for the verb.

Good Use of Adverbs

Although adverbs add description to your writing, they also may present some usage traps. To make sure your writing says what you want it to say, check it for the following adverb usage mistakes.

Adverbs,
page 54.

Placement of Adverbs. Take a good look at where you placed adverbs in your sentences. Moving an adverb can give the sentence a meaning you hadn't intended.

> Her performance *only* pleased the coach.
> (*The coach was no more than pleased by it.*)

> Her performance pleased *only* the coach.
> (*Here,* only *is an adjective that means no one but the coach liked her performance.*)

Place adverbs like *almost, just,* and *only* close to the words they modify.

Comparison of Adverbs. Like adjectives, adverbs come in three "strengths."

Positive	Comparative	Superlative
tenderly	more tenderly	most tenderly
near	nearer	nearest
soon	sooner	soonest
much	more	most
well	better	best

Adverbs usually form the comparative with *more* and the superlative with *most*. Some adverbs follow the adjective pattern of *-er* and *-est*. Others are irregular and don't follow either pattern.

Adverb or Adjective? Some words can be used as either adjectives or adverbs. Among them are the following:

> deep, far, hard, little, long, near, right, straight, close, daily, first, hard, high, late, only, tight

If one of these words modifies a noun, it is an adjective. If it modifies a verb, adjective, or adverb, it is an adverb. To decide, see what question it answers.

> **Adverb** Shana arrived home *late.* (When?)
>
> **Adjective** She had a *late* class. (What kind?)

Some state-of-being verbs, such as *taste* and *feel*, may cause problems because they also can be action verbs. When they are action verbs, it is correct to use an adverb after them.

> Because she had never seen the food before, she tasted it *hesitantly.*

When they are used as state-of-being verbs, you need to use an adjective.

> **Before** This chicken tastes terribly.

> **After** This chicken tastes *terrible.*

In the first sentence, the writer used an adverb (*terribly*) instead of an adjective (*terrible*). This means that the chicken is tasting something—but not doing a very good job of it. In the second sentence, a person is eating the chicken—and finding it very unappetizing.

Editing
85

✔ Checking Mechanics

The **mechanics** of writing include rules for the use of capital letters and punctuation marks, such as periods, commas, and quotation marks. They are like road signs to your readers, telling them what is coming up next and how ideas fit together. Mechanics help your readers have a clearer idea of what you are saying.

Capitalization

Capital letters are signs that something special is coming up next. They tell readers that the next word could be a name, a title, an organization, or the beginning of a new sentence. The following list explains the nouns, pronouns, adjectives, or other words that should begin with capital letters.

Words to Capitalize	Examples
Proper nouns	Fran Brown, Thanksgiving, Mexico, Mississippi River
Proper adjectives	Japanese art, Greek drama
The pronoun *I*	Kate and I rode home.
Names that show a relationship, when used instead of a name or as part of a name	Sam saw Uncle Charles. Dad and Mom told us. *but* My dad and mom told us.
Nicknames and other identifying names	Alexander the Great, Skinny Watson
Special titles when they come right before a name, but not elsewhere, except that *President* is always capitalized when it refers to the head of the United States	Governor Richards, President Clinton *but* She was governor. The President's official residence is the White House.
Brand names	Nike (shoes), Levi's (jeans)
Political and geographic locations and their adjective forms	New York, Brown County, Latin America, Latin American
Nationalities, races, and tribes	Inuit, Apache, Nordic, African American, Korean
Direction words, when part of a specific place name	South Pole, the West, Middle East
Geographic features and common nouns that are part of their names	Lake Michigan, Rocky Mountains, Great Plains *but* We crossed the plains.
Names of buildings, streets, parks, bridges, and other locations, and common nouns that are part of their names	Pentagon, Lincoln Park, George Washington Bridge, Oak Street, U.S. Route 66

Editing
86

Words to Capitalize	Examples
Names of organizations, companies, and institutions	Operation Push, Hanson Sporting Goods, Jefferson High School
Cultural and historical events, wars, treaties, laws, and documents	World War I, Civil War, Declaration of Independence, Treaty of Versailles
Specific awards and prizes	Nobel Peace Prize, Academy Award
Names of trains, planes, ships, and satellites	*Orient Express, Skylab, Voyager 2*
Stars, planets, and constellations	Big Dipper, Arcturus, Milky Way, Earth, Mars **but** the earth, the sun, the moon
Days, months, and holidays, but not seasons	Thursday, June, Fourth of July, spring, summer
First word of a sentence or word that stands alone in place of a sentence	Summer is coming. Wow!
First word of a direct quotation	Jerry said, "Never will I try that again."
First word of salutation and first word of complimentary close of a letter	Dear Ms. Emerson, Yours truly,
The first word, last word, and all important words of titles of books, movies, poems, TV shows, plays, newspapers, magazines, and other writings	*A Tale of Two Cities, Home Alone, The New York Times, Sports Illustrated,* "The Six O'Clock News"
Parts of a book when mentioned elsewhere in the book	See "Volcanoes" in Chapter 3 for more information.

Punctuation

Punctuation marks are the signposts that direct a reader. Imagine a sentence without any punctuation marks:

> **Before** Simply ridiculous said Cecil I wont have anything to do with it

> **After** "Simply ridiculous," said Cecil. "I won't have anything to do with it!"

When you talk, you naturally put in all the pauses and stresses that make your meaning clear. When you write, you need to use punctuation marks to do the same.

Where to Use Periods	Examples
At the ends of declarative sentences	Raul took his new dog to obedience school.

After numbers and letters in an outline	Dog Training
	I. Know your dog well
	  A. Spend time together
	    1. Play

After initials, abbreviations, and parts of abbreviations, *except* for initials of many organizations and for two-letter abbreviations of state names	Ms., Dr., etc., U.S.A. *but* NFL, YMCA, CBS, NY, IL, WY

Where to Use Exclamation Points	Examples
After a word, phrase, or sentence that shows strong feeling	He'll never learn!
To stress a command or strong opinion	Lucky, sit! That's a good dog!
To show that someone is amused, surprised, or upset, or does not believe what is being said	He's all tangled up in the leash! Oh, he'll catch on soon!

Where to Use Question Marks	Examples
At the end of direct questions *but not* with indirect questions	Do you think Lucky will ever be trained? We'll see about that, won't we? *but* They wondered who the new boy was.

Where to Use Colons	Examples
After a complete sentence that leads into a list	Lucky has learned several commands: come, sit, heel, stay, and down.
After the salutation in a business letter	Dear Professor Ely:
Between hours and minutes	Lucky woke me at 5:30 this morning.

Where to Use Semicolons	Examples
Between parts of a compound sentence when they are not joined by a conjunction	Lucky did very well; Toby did even better.
Before words like *hence, however, nevertheless, therefore,* and *thus* when they connect two independent clauses	Flash bit another dog; therefore, he had to leave the class.
To separate items in a list that has commas between the individual items	Graduating were Tuck, Cindy's dog; Toby, Luci's dog; and Lucky, Raul's dog.

Where to Use Dashes	Examples
To indicate a sudden change or break in thought	I was just saying—hey, where are you going?
To stress a part of a sentence	It wasn't easy but she did it—all by herself.
Before a summarizing statement beginning with a word like *all* or *this*	Leash, comb, brush, collar—all these are new expenses.

Where to Use Commas	Examples
To separate the two or more independent clauses that make up a compound sentence	Raul is not sorry he started the class, but he is looking forward to the end of it.
Between words, phrases, or clauses in a series	Lucky barked, whined, and whimpered. Raul tossed the ball, Lucky jumped for it, and Toby caught it.
To set off phrases and dependent clauses that come before the independent clause in a sentence	If he practices a lot, Lucky may be ready for the next class.
To set off phrases, clauses, or appositives that are not essential to the meaning of a sentence (An **appositive** is a word or group of words that means the same thing.)	Luci, Toby's owner, laughed aloud. Raul, upset as he was, managed to smile.
Between parts of a sentence that compare or contrast	The more he whines, the less he learns.
To separate words that might be read together by mistake	Soon after, Luci saw the dog chase a squirrel.
To set off words that introduce a sentence or break the thought	Oh, that was unexpected. She stopped smiling, however, when her friend frowned.
To set off the name of a person spoken to	Why are you laughing, Luci?
To set off the words someone says aloud	"Nothing," said Luci.
After the salutation of a personal letter and complimentary close of any letter	Dear Aunt Lucille, With love,
To separate parts of a date, address, or location	December 12, 1995 17 James Street, Apt. 1B Bloomfield, Mo.
To set off groups of three places in large numbers	10,592; 13,296,155
To separate unrelated numbers in a sentence	In 1994, 200 dogs were trained

Editing
90

Where to Use Apostrophes	Examples
To form the possessive of a noun, but not the possessive of pronouns	Toby's collar, the dog's owner, the dogs' owners *but* theirs, hers, ours, his, its, yours
In place of letters or numbers that have been left out, as in contractions	can't, won't, we'll, class of '98
To show plurals of numbers, letters, or words that are being discussed as words	several *10*'s, all *A*'s How many *the*'s?

Where to Use Hyphens	Examples
In spelling out compound numbers from 21 to 99	thirty-seven
To avoid confusion of words that are spelled alike	re-cover the chair, recover from the flu
After a prefix, when the root word begins with a capital	pre-Renaissance anti-American
In some compound words (Different dictionaries will show different hyphenation. To be consistent, check all compound words in the same dictionary.)	fly-fishing, air-condition
To divide a word at the end of a line (Use a dictionary to find out where you can divide a word.)	Toby found it remark- ably boring.

Editing
91

Where to Use Parentheses	Examples
To enclose words in a sentence that explain something that is not necessary to the sentence's meaning	Emily Dickinson (1830-1886) wrote more than 1,700 poems.
Around numbers or letters that show divisions in a sentence	In order, her choices are (1) math, (2) art, and (3) music.

Where to Use Quotation Marks	Examples
To enclose all of a **direct quotation** (the exact words someone says or writes)	"Chandra's going to space camp," Troy said, "if she can get a scholarship."
To enclose quoted words or phrases in a sentence	Chandra's mom tells her she's "as wild as a colt."
Use single quotation marks to enclose a quote within a quote	"My mom told me, 'You're as wild as a colt,'" Chandra said.
To enclose the titles of poems and short musical pieces	"Mother to Son," "Birches," "Star-Spangled Banner"
Around the titles of lectures, sermons, pamphlets, chapters of books, and magazine articles	"How to Build a Birdhouse"

Where to Use Italics	Examples
You may use either *italics* (slanted type) or <u>underlining</u> in these places	
For any words, letters, or numbers considered as words	*A, and,* and *the* are articles. Write *t* for true. Be sure you write your *7*'s clearly.
For the titles of books, plays, long poems, magazines, and newspapers newspapers	*James and the Giant Peach, Seventeen, Los Angeles Times*
For titles of paintings and other works of art	*American Gothic, Mona Lisa, David*
For names of specific spacecraft, planes, trains, and satellites	*City of New Orleans, Spirit of St. Louis, Mariner 4*

Where to Use Virgules	Examples
As a dividing line between dates, fractions, and abbreviations	10/20/95 1/2 c/o (in care of)
To show where a line of poetry ends when it is not shown line for line	"What goes up,/ Must come down."/ Said the juggler/ To the clown.

Where to Use Ellipses	Examples
With direct quotes to show that a word (or words) was omitted	Mr. Hanes said, "I won't answer now . . . or later."
With direct quotes to show that a sentence (or sentences) was omitted	The book began: "We thought the rainbow promised a good day's travel, . . . but it proved misleading."
To indicate words omitted at the end of a sentence (Use end-of-sentence punctuation followed by the ellipses.)	Jody asked, "When will we get there? . . . "

Proofreader's Marks

⌐H New paragraph

⌐ New line   fruit⌐vegetables⌐milk

Put a space in here   When I went#to

≡ Capitalize a small letter   george≡

/ Make a capital letter lower-case   /Wintertime

⊙ Put a period here   I went home⊙

⌒ Put a comma here   Julio⌒ Mickey⌒ and Luis

∧ Put this letter or word (or these letters or words) here   a my Tht is house. ∧ ∧

— Get rid of this word (or these words)   ~~many~~ one horse

∿ Have this letter (or word) change places with this letter (or word or words)   Th∿er breakfast∿not is∿ ready.

Editing Checklist

The Editing Checklist is a guide for checking your revision. Look over the list and decide which of the items you need to check. Remember that your ideas show through the window of your writing. You're clearing away any last smudges on the glass.

Will readers be able to read my words?

- [ ] check spelling
- [ ] look up compound words
- [ ] check for correct homophone spelling

Will readers be confused by sudden changes in direction?

- [ ] check for consistent verb tense
- [ ] check for consistent use of first or third person
- [ ] check for consistent use of singular or plural

Will readers be able to follow my sentences?

- [ ] make sure subjects and verbs agree
- [ ] make sure pronouns and antecedents agree
- [ ] fix sentence fragments
- [ ] rewrite run-on sentences
- [ ] check for modifier problems
- [ ] rewrite to make parallel expressions

Do I have any errors in the use of parts of speech?

☐ look for use of the right forms of pronouns

☐ check for good use of adjectives—placement, forms of comparison, use after linking verbs

☐ check for good use of verbs—active voice, tense

☐ check for good use of adverbs—placement, forms of comparison, adverb rather than adjective form

Did I use the correct mechanics signals?

Editing
95

☐ include correct capitalization

☐ include correct punctuation

periods

exclamation points

question marks

colons

semicolons

dashes

commas

apostrophes

hyphens

parentheses

quotation marks

italics

virgules

ellipses

CHAPTER FIVE

SHARING
AND PUBLISHING

When you are ready to share your writing, you need to make a clear, fresh copy called a **final manuscript.**

Creating a Final Manuscript

To create a final manuscript, type your work or copy it clearly by hand.

○ Leave margins on the top, bottom, and sides of a page.

○ Number the pages at the top or bottom.

○ Be sure not to skip any material when you are writing it over.

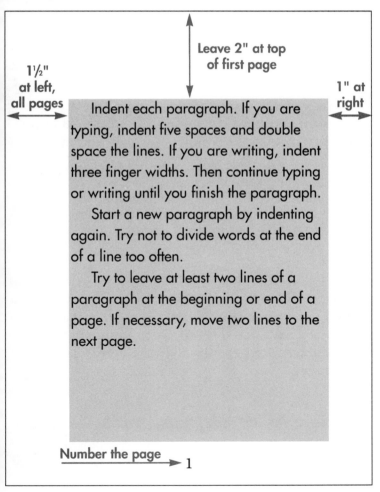

Leave 2" at top of first page

1½" at left, all pages

1" at right

Indent each paragraph. If you are typing, indent five spaces and double space the lines. If you are writing, indent three finger widths. Then continue typing or writing until you finish the paragraph.

Start a new paragraph by indenting again. Try not to divide words at the end of a line too often.

Try to leave at least two lines of a paragraph at the beginning or end of a page. If necessary, move two lines to the next page.

Number the page → 1

When you've finished making the clean copy, read it against your edited manuscript. Did you leave anything out (words, sentences, paragraphs, punctuation, etc.)?

Reading Your Writing Aloud

No matter how old you are, it's always exciting to hear good pieces of writing read aloud. Even people who don't enjoy reading enjoy being read to. What does the reader do to draw listeners into the piece? You will notice three things right away:

- The reader speaks clearly and smoothly.
- The reader varies his or her tone of voice.
- The reader stresses certain words.

If the reader spoke every word the same way, it would put listeners to sleep. To read a story well, you need to practice reading aloud. First, read the story to yourself so that you know when to separate your sentences with pauses and stress important words. Read the following words silently:

> I was never so scared as when I took my final exam in lifesaving. There was my instructor struggling in the water. Could I save her? Sure enough, she was close to the edge of the pool. If I could just extend a pole to her. . . .

Now try reading the sentences aloud. Since you've read them silently, you know what words to stress. You can stress words either by raising or lowering your voice. As you read, notice how your tone of voice can help the listeners understand your story.

Sharing Your Writing with Others

You probably would like others to read or hear your writing—but when, how, and in what form? There

are many possibilities. You can publish it in a class-room book or local newspaper or read it aloud to classmates. You can make a tape and donate copies of the tape to the public library, school library, and teachers in the school. You can enter your work in a contest. You even might make copies to send to all your relatives on a special occasion.

Starting a Writing Group

Another way to share your writing is by forming a small writing group. In such a group, you see other writers' work and hear what they have to say about yours. If you begin a writing group, have members take turns reading their work out loud. Members should listen carefully and encourage each other by giving positive advice for improving the work.

Publishing in Books or Magazines

Have you written a script for a movie? Have you written a poem? The librarian can help you locate a place to send it by looking in a reference book such as *Writer's Market.* In it you will find information about magazines and book publishers—even the names of editors to whom to send your work. If you try this, however, keep in mind that even famous authors have collected many rejection slips. Those are the letters that begin:

> Dear Friend,
>
> Thank you for submitting your poem to us. It does not match our publishing needs at this time.

Publishing by Yourself

☞ **Japanese Bookbinding, page 120.**

Many writers have begun by publishing their works themselves. You need only a typewriter or computer and the chance to use a photocopying machine. You may want to get together with other writers to publish your own magazine. Make copies and sell them door to door, give them away at the supermarket, distribute them at a scout meeting, or ask the school librarian if you could put a copy in the school library. If you think younger readers might like your story, ask the teacher of a lower grade if you could give the book or magazine to that classroom.

You could send copies of a story (or essay or poem) to all your relatives at Thanksgiving. You might interview a grandparent and write his or her life story in your own words. Then give the story to all the members of your family and to the local historical society. Before you know it, your writing will reach many readers. Your writing is one of the best gifts you can give.

CHAPTER SIX

WRITING FOR
SCHOOL

Writing a Short Report

When you first entered school, your teachers may have answered most of your questions for you. But as you grow older, your teachers will expect you to find the answers to many questions yourself. Finding and putting together information about a subject in a short, written report will become more and more important as you advance through school.

A **short report** is a brief piece of writing that combines information on a single subject from books, magazines, and other sources of information. Most short reports are from 375 to 625 words long. This usually comes to 1½ to 2½ pages if the report is typed.

Writing a report is like writing a story or any other piece—you follow the same process. Using this step-by-step approach can reduce the assignment to smaller, easier tasks.

☞ **A Look at the Writing Process, pages 1–3.**

Planning

The first step in writing your report is to be sure you understand the assignment. Before deciding on a topic, you should be sure you are free to choose your topic. Perhaps your teacher wants you to select a topic from a list or to report on something you studied in class. Overlooking this important part of the assignment can cause you to waste a lot of time.

You also need to think about the purpose of the report your teacher has assigned. Are you expected to describe something or explain how something works? Such reports are called **summary reports** because your report summarizes information without telling how you feel about it.

There are many possible ways to report on a particular topic. For example, suppose you are interested in dolphins. You could write a summary report on one of the following subjects:

Dolphins

Explain
The difference between dolphins and whales
How dolphins communicate
The biggest threats to the survival of dolphins

Describe
The various types of dolphins
How dolphins are trained
How dolphins care for each other

It is also important to think about who will be reading your report. Will you be sharing your report with classmates? If so, you'll want to include information that interests and excites them and to avoid repeating facts they already know.

Also, be sure you understand how long the report should be. If you're asked to write a 500-word report, don't try to write exactly 500 words. If your report runs a little short or a little long, your teacher won't mind. But, if the report runs very short, don't try to stretch it out by just adding more words. This will only make the report dull and empty, and it won't fool your teacher! You will need to look up and add more information to complete your report.

Choosing Your Topic. Deciding on your topic is one of the most important parts of planning your report. You'll want to select a topic that interests you and your audience.

Very often a topic you already know something about makes a good subject for a report. It usually means you're interested in the subject and anxious to tell others about it. One way to help you decide on possible subjects for your report is to make an interest inventory. An inventory is simply a list. So an **interest inventory** is a list of things that interest you. It might include one or more of the following:

School
104

- favorite subjects in school
- hobbies
- types of magazines or books you read
- some people you admire

Another way to decide on a topic is to browse through an encyclopedia or almanac. Do any of the articles hold a special interest for you? Which ones would you like to know more about?

☞ Finding Information for Your Report, pages 106–107.

Before deciding on your topic, it's a good idea to do some background reading on the subject. An article in an encyclopedia or similar reference book is a good place to start. An **encyclopedia** is a book or set of books containing articles on thousands of subjects. Some encyclopedias are limited to a particular area, such as science. Within an encyclopedia information is arranged in alphabetical order. Encyclopedia articles will give you some ideas for approaching the subject. If you checked an encyclopedia article on dolphins, for example, you'd probably learn that dolphins have an unusual ability to communicate, that there are many types of dolphins, and that many dolphins have died in fishing nets. A report on any of these topics could be very interesting.

Once you've thought about your interests and done some background reading, you should be able to list several possible topics for a short report. Then you need to ask yourself the following questions:

 Is the topic the right size for a short report? Can the subject be covered in a few pages (or in whatever length you need)?

 Do I have enough time to find the information needed to do this report? Is the topic too large and complicated for a short report?

 Can I find enough information about this subject in the library? Will there be books and magazine articles on this topic?

Limiting Your Topic. A good report will not try to cover too much or too little. Sometimes students are afraid of running out of things to say in a report. As a result, many reports make the mistake of trying to cover a topic that is too big.

One good way to go about limiting your topic is to begin with a broad, general topic. Then, as you read some articles on the subject, you can decide what part of the broad topic would be most interesting to write about. For example, suppose you started with this broad topic:

General Topic: Dolphins

To cover such a large topic, you'd have to write a book. You'd need to include information on the many types of dolphins, their appearance, and their behavior. Also, you'd need to include something about their chances for survival, their eating habits, and perhaps recent research on dolphins. If your topic is too general, you will try to include everything in your report. But in the end, however, you'll be able to tell very little about any one part of the topic.

☞ **Narrowing Your Topic, page 18.**

You must narrow your topic to something you can expect to cover in a few pages. By asking questions, you can often narrow your subject.

> **General Topic:** Dolphins
> **Ask:** What part of this subject would be most interesting?
> **Limited Topic:** How dolphins communicate
>
> **General Topic:** Civil rights leaders
> **Ask:** What person or group is a good example of this subject?
> **Limited Topic:** Rosa Parks' contribution to the civil rights movement
>
> **General Topic:** The American Revolution
> **Ask:** What brief period of time would be most interesting?
> **Limited Topic:** Washington's winter at Valley Forge

Continue asking questions and narrowing your focus until you have a topic that you can cover in a short report.

When you're finished you should be able to state your topic in a phrase or sentence. Then list some questions you expect to answer in your report.

> How dolphins communicate
> Do dolphins communicate like people?
> Can dolphins be taught certain words?
> Can dolphins communicate with each other?

Finding Information for Your Report. The process of finding information for your report really begins with the background reading you do when choosing and limiting a topic.

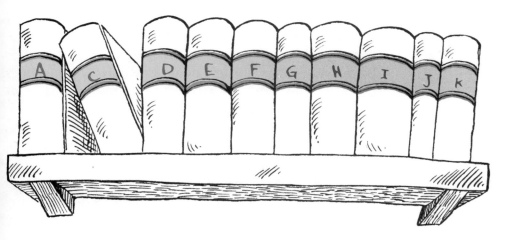

Perhaps you want to consult an encyclopedia. Most of the longer articles in an encyclopedia contain headings that allow you to pick out the particular information you'd like to check. In some encyclopedias, the longer articles include some references to other books and articles on the subject.

Other general reference books include the following:

atlas
a book of maps that sometimes includes information about geography, climate, and population

almanac
an annual book or calendar giving information about weather, historical events, government leaders, or awards and record holders in sports or other fields

biographical reference
A book about famous people of today and long ago, for example *Who's Who of American Women* and *Who's Who among Black Americans,* that has information about their birth dates and birth places, major events in their lives, awards won, etc.

Reference books are usually kept separate from other books in the library. You can't check these books out of the library, so you must use them in the reference area. Be sure to bring note cards and a pen or pencil so you can write down any information from these sources that you'll want to use later.

The **card catalog** contains a list of the books and other materials that can be found in the library. It's an important tool for helping you find information on a topic.

Most card catalogs are found in a cabinet of small file drawers. The catalog usually has three cards for each book: the author card, the title card, and the subject card. Because each title is cataloged in three different ways, you can look for information using an author's name, the title of a book, or the subject you want information about. Some libraries use a separate set of cabinets for each type of card. The cards are filed in the card catalog in alphabetical order. Most librarians keep scratch paper and pencils next to the card catalog so that you can copy information from the cards.

Author Card

> **599.53**
> **DON**
>> Donoghue, Michael
>> Save the dolphins
>> Sheridan House, 1990
>> 119 p. illus

Title Card

> **599.53**
> **DON**
>> Save the dolphins
>> Donoghue, Michael
>> Save the dolphins
>> Sheridan House, 1990
>> 119 p. illus

Subject Card

> **599.53**
> **DON**
>> Dolphin
>> Donoghue, Michael
>> Save the dolphins
>> Sheridan House, 1990
>> 119 p. illus
> See also porpoise.

Note that the subject cards may list references to other subject cards in the card catalog. For example, if you are trying to find information about dolphins, you could also check under the subject *porpoise.*

Author cards are alphabetized by the author's last name. Title cards, however, are filed by the second word in the title if the first word is *A, An,* or *The.* For example, *The Playful Dolphins* by Julia Wood would be listed under *W* (Wood) on the author card and under *P* (Playful) on the title card.

The **call number** in the upper-left corner of each card tells you how to find the book in the library. Each book has a different number. The call number will match the number on the spine, or edge, of the book. Most libraries have a guide or map showing you where books with various numbers are found.

```
Welcome to the Lincoln School Library
         Computer Card Catalog

You may search the catalog using one
 of the methods below. Choose by
pressing the correct key. You can
get help by pressing the HELP key.


To search by        [1] subject
                     [2] author
                     [3] title
                     [4] all categories
```

Some libraries now have their card catalogs on computer. The computerized catalogs use the same system as the cards. To use a computer catalog, simply follow the directions on the screen. If you have a problem, ask a librarian for help.

To find magazine articles on your topic, try looking in *The Readers' Guide to Periodical Literature.* This source lists articles published in more than 175 magazines. It gives the names of the magazines in which the articles appear and lists each article by author and subject.

DOLLS

See also

Baby Alive dolls
Kammer & Reinhardt
Margaret Steiff GmbH

Barbie, meet Brenda [Mattel dolls based on TV show Beverly Hills, 90210] T. Gliatto. il *People Weekly* 37:120–1 F 17 '92

Collectors and collecting

Kammer & Reinhardt: dollmakers of verve & variety. M. Jailer, il *Antiques & Collecting Hobbies* 97:30–1 Mr '92
The traditional dolls of Japan. M. Jailer. il *Antiques & Collecting Hobbies* 96:58–9 Ja '92

DOLNICK, EDWARD

Why women live longer than men. *Reader's Digest* 140:157–60 Ja '92

DOLPHINS

Playful genius of the sea. P. O. D'Aulaire and E. D'Aulaire, il *Reader's Digest* 140:54–9 '92

DOME STADIUMS *See* Stadiums

The *Readers' Guide* is published twenty-one times a year. This makes it possible for you to find very recent articles—even those printed just last month.

To find an article on your topic, begin with the most recent issue of *Readers' Guide.* Then, work backward to find more information. Issues from previous years are usually combined into one book. This way you need to check only one book for an entire year's articles.

When you find an article you think you'd like to read, write down the title of the article and the name of the magazine with its date and volume number. Look in the front of *Readers' Guide* for an explanation of any abbreviations.

Some libraries can search computer databases for articles. These systems can offer indexes, summaries of articles, or the entire article. Computer searches are quicker and more convenient than searching *Readers' Guide.* However, libraries may charge for this service. Your librarian will help you with computer searches.

Taking Notes. Take clear, exact notes as you read through your resources. This is important for two reasons: First, you need to keep a record of the books and magazines you use so you can prepare a bibliography. (A **bibliography** is a list of books and magazines you used in making your report.) Second, you want to save the information and quotations that will be most helpful.

Make a bibliography card for each source of information you plan to include in your report. A **bibliography card** lists the author, title, city (and state or country, if necessary) of publication, publisher, date, and page numbers. You will use this information later when you prepare your bibliography.

Preparing the
Bibliography,
page 116.

Patent, Dorothy Hinshaw.
Dolphins and Porpoises.
New York: Holiday House, 1987.

D'Aulaire, P.O. and E.D'Aulaire.
"Playful Genius of the Sea."
Reader's Digest,
March 1992, pp 54-59.

Use a second set of cards to make notes on the main points or to copy quotations you may want to use in your report. These cards are called **note cards.** Write the notes in your own words. If you want to use an author's exact words, use quotation marks. Write only one idea or quotation on each note card. This way you can rearrange your notes as you organize your report.

Each note card should contain three kinds of information:

     a heading to show what kind of information is on the card

     a short description of the source of the information, including the page number

     a summary of the information or a direct quotation

Note Card

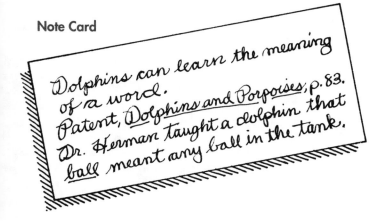

Dolphins can learn the meaning of a word.
Patent, *Dolphins and Porpoises*, p. 83.
Dr. Herman taught a dolphin that *ball* meant any ball in the tank.

Organizing Your Information. Before beginning to write your report, make a chart or map or make a topic outline of your report. A **topic outline** is a list of short phrases that give the framework or skeleton of your report. Having a topic outline will make it easier for you to write the draft.

One good way to go about making an outline is to look at the questions you wrote about your topic when you planned your report. You may find that you have added or dropped some questions as you found information about your topic. Divide your note cards into groups that go with each question.

Next, change each question into a topic and list the information you found under each topic. Your topic outline will have main topics and subtopics. The **main topics** identify the large parts of the report. They are marked with a Roman numeral. The **subtopics** are the details or facts that explain the main topics. They are marked with capital letters.

On the next page, you can see how the answers to the questions on how dolphins communicate (page 106) can be turned into an outline.

Getting Ideas from Charting; Mapping, pages 16–17.

I. Dolphins respond to sounds
   A. Not like human words
   B. True language is learned
      1. Recent research
      2. How scientists think dolphins learn language

II. Scientists have taught dolphins words and sentences.
   A. Dolphins respond to sounds and hand signals.
      1. Methods of teaching dolphins
      2. Examples of hand signals
   B. Dolphins understand words used together in different ways.

III. Don't know if dolphins can use language themselves

School

114

☞ **Thesis
sentence,
page 23.**

Writing the Thesis Sentence. After you finish your topic outline, you should be able to write a thesis sentence. A thesis sentence tells the main idea of the report in one sentence. Because it helps you and your reader focus on the main idea of your report, the thesis sentence is often the first sentence in the report. A thesis sentence for the report on dolphins might be "Dolphins communicate more than most animals but not as well as humans."

Drafting

When you've finished all of your planning, you are ready to write your draft. You should put away the books and magazines and use your outline and your notes. Remember, if you use a quotation—the author's exact words—put it in quotation marks. Write on every other line to leave room for changes you'll want to make later.

Follow your outline as you write to make sure that you include all your ideas. Write down everything you have to say without stopping to correct spelling, punctuation, or usage. You'll have the chance to add, take out, or reorder information when you revise. And you'll be able to correct grammatical errors as you edit.

Revising

If possible, put your first draft aside for a day before revising it. This will help you imagine you are a reader looking at it for the first time.

When you revise your report, see if you've said what you want to say. Also, check to see that you've said it clearly. As you read through your draft, ask yourself these questions:

⌕ Have I followed the main sections and sub-sections in my topic outline?

⌕ Is the report easy to follow? Are any parts unclear or confusing?

⌕ Do all the facts and information tell about the thesis sentence?

⌕ Can any sentences be improved by shortening them or combining them with other sentences?

Sometimes it helps to read your report to a friend or family member and have that person make suggestions.

Revision ☞ Checklist, page 58.

Editing and Assembling the Final Report

When you've finished revising your report, you're ready to begin correcting mistakes in usage, punctuation, and spelling. One good way to check for mistakes is to use an editing checklist. Read through your report several times. Each time, look for a particular item on the checklist.

Editing ☞ Checklist, pages 94–95.

Preparing the Final Copy. When you're sure you've said what you want to say clearly and correctly, make a neat final copy. Sometimes your teacher will tell how the final copy should be prepared.

If you have no special instructions, reports should follow certain guidelines. If you type, your report should be on typing paper. Avoid hyphenating words at the bottom of a page. If you divide a paragraph between two pages, try not to leave only one line on a page.

Creating ☞ a Final Manuscript, page 97.

Give your report an interesting title. If your teacher requires it, make a title page that includes the title, your name, and any other information you need, such as your teacher's name, the date, and the class. Attach the title page to the front of your report.

Preparing the Bibliography. The bibliography goes on a separate page at the end of your report. For each book or magazine that provided information you used in your report, give the author, title, and certain facts about the publisher. Study the following sample bibliography.

> D'Aulaire, P.O., and D'Aulaire, E. "Playful Genius of the Sea." Reader's Digest. March 1992, pp. 54–59.
>
> Patent, Dorothy Hinshaw. Dolphins and Porpoises. New York: Holiday House, 1987.

☞ **Where to Use Quotation Marks; Italics,** page 92. Each item is alphabetized by the author's last name. The title of a book or magazine is underlined or italicized and followed by a period. Put quotation marks around titles of articles from magazines. The publisher's name, city of publication, and date of publication are given and punctuated as shown in the sample.

Answering Essay Questions

To answer some test questions, you may have to write an **essay.** That is, you must write one or more paragraphs to answer the question. Essay tests measure whether you can combine and organize information and ideas. They also test whether you can express yourself clearly in writing. Some tests give you a chance to express your own ideas about a subject.

Like other types of writing, your answers to an essay question should include complete sentences and paragraphs. They also should be carefully planned and well organized.

The most important thing about answering an essay question is to be sure you understand the question. You must do exactly what the question asks. Essay questions have a key word—usually the verb—that tells you what you must do. You may be asked to analyze, compare, define, describe, explain, or summarize. To do this, you need to know the meaning of these verbs.

Verb	Meaning	Example
analyze	examine closely; break into parts and show how the parts are connected	Analyze the water cycle and show how aquifers fit into it.
compare *or* compare and contrast	show how things are alike or are alike and different	Compare football with soccer.
define	give an exact meaning	Define *ecosystem*.
describe	tell about something in detail	Describe how to start a campfire safely.
explain	give reasons or causes for something or tell how something works	Explain how a fan cools you.
summarize	give the main points	Summarize the War of 1812.

Once you are sure you understand the question, you can begin to plan your answer. Use the steps of the writing process.

Planning

☞ Organizing Your Information, pages 113–114.

One good way to begin is to outline the main points you want to include in your answer. Then number the items to show the order in which you plan to discuss each point. If new ideas occur to you as you write, jot them down in the margin so you don't forget them.

School
118

Drafting

☞ Thesis sentence, page 23.

Try to write a thesis sentence that summarizes your answer. Then try to think of new examples to support your thesis. Be sure all the information you include is covered by your thesis sentence. Do not include any information that does not support your thesis sentence.

If you express an opinion, be sure to give reasons for it. Your reasons are the important part of the answer because they support your opinion.

Don't leave out information because you think your teacher knows that you know it. Even simple information can often be related to other material. This will show your teacher that you understand the subject.

Even if you're not sure of the answer, write *something*. If you have a hunch about the answer, write it out. It's better to write your best ideas than to give no answer at all.

If you're running out of time, quickly outline the rest of your answer. You may not get full credit, but getting partial credit is better than none at all.

Revising

Leave some space after each answer. If you think of something later, you'll have room to add it. Usually, your teacher will allow you to draw an arrow to show where the new information fits in.

Editing

When you've finished, reread your answer. Check your spelling, punctuation, and usage.

Sharing

Of course, the sharing step is just handing in your paper. Good luck!

1. To make the front and back covers, cut two pieces of heavy paper the same size as your pages.

2. Lightly draw a straight line about ½ inch from the left edge of the front cover. Mark dots every ½ inch or so along the line. Put your papers between the covers, and clip everything together on the right edge so nothing slips.

3. Use a sharp tool to punch holes through the dots. Make sure your holes go through all the layers. Turn the book so that the spine is at the top, and the back cover is facing you.

4. Thread a large needle with yarn that is five times the length of the cover. Don't knot the end or double the yarn. Push the threaded needle from the back cover through the first hole, leaving about a four-inch "tail" that you will use to tie your binding in Step 5. Wrap the yarn over the top edge and go back through the same hole. Now pull the needle through the front of the next hole, and again wrap the yarn over the top edge and go back through the same hole. Repeat these steps until you reach the last hole on the right.

5. Wrap the yarn around the right edge. Then sew straight back across the line—in one hole and out the next. All spaces should now be filled. Wrap the yarn around the left end and tie it in the back to the "tail" you left in Step 4. Cut off any extra yarn. Crease your cover at the yarn line.

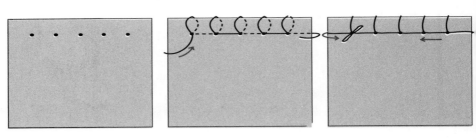